OUR CHURCH

OUR CHURCH

A guide to the Kirk of Scotland

R D Kernohan

THE SAINT ANDREW PRESS : EDINBURGH

First published in 1985 by
THE SAINT ANDREW PRESS
121 George Street, Edinburgh

Copyright © 1985 R D Kernohan

ISBN 0 7152 0587 0

British Library Cataloguing in Publication Data
Kernohan, R D
  Our Church: a guide to the Kirk of Scotland.
  1. Church of Scotland
  I. Title
  285'.2411   BX9072

ISBN 0 7152 0587 0

Printed in Great Britain by
Holmes McDougall Ltd, Edinburgh, Scotland

Contents

Acknowledgments

The Publishers gratefully acknowledge and thank the following individuals and organisations for their kind permission to reproduce the illustrations in this book:

Aberdeen Art Gallery and Museums: 31

Audio-Visual Unit, Department of Communication, Church of Scotland: 63

Board of World Mission and Unity, Church of Scotland: 80, 93, 94, 95 (all)

Alan Buchan: 37

Graham Galloway: Cover and book design

Revd Alan Knox: 75 (above, right)

Life and Work, Church of Scotland: 9, 19, 47 (below), 52 (below), 60, 89, 104

National Galleries of Scotland, Edinburgh: 33

New College Library, Edinburgh: 40 (both), 41

Revd Roland Portchmouth: 13, 18, 27, 35, 48 (above), 69, 77

Press Office, Department of Communication, Church of Scotland: 65, 67, 79

Publicity Office, Department of Communication, Church of Scotland: 28, 73, 75 (above left, below left, below right), 83, 84

Bryan Ross: 20, 48 (below), 51, 54, 59, 70

William Ross: 45

Royal Commission on Ancient Monuments, Scotland: 44, 47 (above), 49 (above), 52 (above), 55, 58
Crown Copyright: Royal Commission on Ancient Monuments, Scotland

Scottish Development Department: 50 (below), 56, 57 (right)
Crown Copyright: reproduced by permission of the Scottish Development Department

Scottish Tourist Board: 46, 49 (below), 50 (above), 53, 57 (left)

John Sheerin, photographer: 23, 40 (both), 41, 80, 94

Lesley Ann Taylor: 17 (both)

Preface

Welcome to our Church

This is a simple guide to the Church of Scotland. It tries to introduce the Scots Kirk, describe it and explain it. It is meant to help everyone who encounters the Church of Scotland, including those who have already had long experience of it. Indeed, many of us who have belonged to it for a long time are still learning new things about it. But perhaps that applies to the whole Church of God and not just His Scottish Presbyterian Kirk.

There are three groups of people for whom this guide may be especially useful and helpful. We want them to get to know our Church and feel welcome in it. First, there are those of you who are thinking of becoming full members of the Church of Scotland, with all the rights and duties which this involves. This group also includes those who are already members, but who do not know much about the Church beyond their own locality. Second, there are those of you who live in Scotland and belong to another denomination, or to no Church at all, yet who realise the significance of the Kirk and Presbyterianism in both Scottish life and Scottish history. Those of us within the Church of Scotland do not always take into consideration how hard it can be for you to understand the procedures and traditions of the Kirk, even the customs which we think of as simple and basic. Third, there are many of you who come into contact with Scotland as visitors or immigrants, whether from other parts of the UK (England, Wales and Ireland), or from overseas. We want you to see the outside of our churches, but we also want to help you see inside the Kirk and see beyond the well-worn (and so often outworn) stereotypes of dour Presbyterians and stern Calvinists. There is such a thing as Scottish reserve, but it is combined with cheerfulness and thankfulness. The Scots extend a warm welcome to both friends and strangers.

If you are interested, you will soon see what a rich variety there is to be found in the parish churches of Scotland, and that there are many different Christian styles and traditions within our Presbyterianism. We are a very comprehensive Church indeed. But this reflects something more fundamental. The Church is an affair of the heart, not just a matter of historic or humdrum buildings. It is still making and living its own history as well as the history of Scotland.

To be fully understood the Church has to be a shared experience. We hope that those of you with whom we can share a little in these pages will want to share a lot more. We want everyone to know that they are welcome not only at our services and the activities of our congregations, but also welcome to share our sense of what the Kirk means to Scotland and what it contributes from Scotland to the universal Church of which it is a part, and of which Jesus Christ was the Founder and is the Head.

The information here is as accurate and up-to-date as we could make it, and the opinions expressed are meant to be objective and well-balanced, particularly on the range of matters where several points of view or different practices are to be found within our Church. We are not a Church where everyone does the same thing or thinks the same way. (However, the opinions and interpretations are the author's. No-one else needs to be blamed for them.)

Welcome to our Church. And, even more important for Christians, welcome to His Church, of which the Scots Kirk is a part.

The Department of Publicity's 'Operation Welcome'

The essence of the Kirk

1

Universal but Scottish

The Church of Scotland is a Protestant part of the catholic (or universal) Church. It has the style, beliefs and traditions that theologians and historians call 'Reformed'. This involves the system of church government usually called in English 'Presbyterian'. The word means that the Church is regulated, not by a hierarchy of individual executive dignitaries, but by a system of councils, committees or courts.

But the Church of Scotland (often abbreviated to 'The Kirk') is Christian first, Reformed second, and Scottish only third. The Kirk's constitution begins by saying that it is part of the holy catholic or universal Church and sets out the basic doctrines of the Christian faith. When the Kirk refers to the 'catholic' Church, it does not mean the Roman Catholic Church under the Pope, nor even the system and tradition of bishops maintained by Anglicans. The Kirk has neither Pope nor bishops, but holds to the 'catholic' faith of the Christian creeds and to the idea of a worldwide or universal Church based on them. Its supreme rule of faith and life is the Bible, for it believes that the Bible must be read and used with all our God-given powers of reason, which should be reverently and humbly brought to the task.

The features which the Church of Scotland has in common with other Christians, from the Salvation Army to Greek Orthodoxy, are more fundamentally important to it than the elements which give it its distinctly Scottish character. It is important to emphasise this fact before proceeding to explain the peculiarly Scottish aspects of the Kirk and the way in which it remains at the heart of so much, both in Scottish history and in modern Scottish life.

Even its Presbyterianism is not distinctively Scottish. Our reformation of the faith, like the first Christian missions to Scotland, showed how international Christianity is. The Reformed or Presbyterian form of the Church came to Scotland after continental European reformers had tried to recapture the spirit and style of the early Mediterranean Church. It was, and still remains, the main form of Protestant Christianity in Holland, Switzerland, France and Hungary. The biggest single personal influence on it was that of the brilliant French intellectual, John Calvin, who worked in Switzerland, and who owed much to the great German reformer, Martin Luther. Similar influences (like that of John Calvin's, so decisive in Scottish Church history) were also important in England, Germany and later in the United States. Today these influences remain very important in Irish and Welsh Protestantism as well as in a worldwide network of Churches influenced by Scots and others, either as immigrants or missionaries.

Important and far-flung though the Scottish influence has been, it is wrong to think of Presbyterianism as being invented and distilled in Scotland and then labelled for export to the rest of the world. It is also wrong

John Calvin 1509-64

Roland Portchmouth

Institutes Christian Religion

to think of the Church of Scotland as having been founded at the time of the Scots Reformation of 1560. It was not founded then but reformed ('re-formed') to bring it closer to the pattern given to the early Church by Jesus's disciples; the same Church which, already changing and evolving in various ways, saints like Ninian and Columba had brought to Scotland.

Our Church in Scotland, like the universal Church, is always changing in outward styles and customs: for example, in its language; its music; its buildings; or even in the acceptable way to dress for church. However, the continuity of the Church is to be found in the way it represents unchanging truths in changing situations. Despite the changes, Jesus remains 'the same yesterday, today, and for ever' *(Hebrews 13:8).*

There are times when the Church is slow to change. But there are other times when it is all too easy, given the changeability of this computer and cable-TV age, to underestimate the importance of history and tradition to a country's way of life. The Church, in a very special way, stands for tradition as well as the inevitability of change. It is itself always changing but, even more important, it is trying to influence people's lives. In Europe particularly, it has become such a significant part of the human heritage that it is impossible fully to appreciate our present situation and future prospects without it. There are also some countries where the character of the nation is intimately and inextricably bound up with the kind of Church or Churches it has: Poland is one obvious example, Scotland is another.

In a very important sense the Church of Scotland is both *our* Church and a part of our nationality and identity in Scotland. This is not only true for the large number of people who belong to it, with their names on the Communion (or membership) rolls of the Kirk's congregations, but it is also true of the larger number who, in a much vaguer sense, think of themselves as Protestant or Presbyterian. It is true even of

those who either adhere to a quite different religious tradition, or consciously reject religion altogether.

The Kirk is a fact of Scottish life and history, and is as clearly a part of Scottish emotion and experience as the church spires are of any view of our cities, towns and country parishes. Spires and church buildings may be important. (Later we shall provide a very basic and general guide to some of the most historic, significant or typically characteristic of them in Scotland.) But people are far more important in the Church, for they *are* the Church.

Opinion polls today reveal that more than 60 per cent of Scots identify themselves in some way with the Church of Scotland, even although just under a third of the babies born in Scotland are now baptised in it. Nearly 900 000 Scots adults are on the Kirk's congregational Communion rolls, although only about 60 per cent of those are usually recorded as attending at least one Communion service a year. More than 46 000 men and women are elders of the Church;

that is to say, members of its kirk sessions (i.e. local church councils). Despite the name, 'elders', it applies to adults of all ages. Furthermore, 40 per cent of those recently ordained have been women.

A Scottish church attendance census taken in 1984 showed that on an 'ordinary' Sunday there were about 266 000 adults attending services in the Kirk's churches, plus 95 000 children, which accounts for just over 70 per cent of all Protestant church attendance in Scotland. Roman Catholics were shown to be more regular attenders, although facing similar trends. Their 18 per cent of Scotland's population provided 40 per cent of its regular church attendance on Sundays. However, even although Kirk members may not get marks for perfect attendance, the census showed that the proportion of all adults attending church regularly (17 per cent) was appreciably higher than in England, or in many European countries.

'And how many priests do you have?' the visitor sometimes asks. Some Presbyterians would answer 'none', but the more correct theological answer would be, 'Just as many as we have Christians'. For the priesthood of all believers is a doctrine basic to Reformed and other Protestant thinking. We do not have an order of priests because we believe that all Christians are ordered to be priests. As the New Testament tells us in its account of the Christians' new song: 'You have made them a kingdom of priests to serve our God.' (*Revelation 5:10*). We do, however, have ministers: about 1500 of them in full-time Church service (mainly in parishes), and several hundred others employed elsewhere. Most ministers are men but, since 1968, women have also been eligible for ministerial ordination. Now a growing minority of parish and other ministers are women.

Strictly speaking, to be a minister means to serve. The special service required of a 'minister of Word and Sacrament' is that he or she preaches, presides at the Lord's Supper (or Communion) and administers the other sacrament, Baptism. In practice, the minister is also the chief local pastor (a specialised chaplain) and very close to being the local executive agent of the Church. One of the complaints now often voiced within the Kirk is that it is 'minister-centred', with both the church services and the church work concentrated upon what the minister says and does. On the other hand, those who complain (often ministers themselves) are not very effective in arranging matters more favourably. And some of the apparent centrality of the ministry probably results from ministers giving very satisfactory specialised service as preachers and pastors. By the standards of other Churches, they preach few bad sermons and probably err nowadays on the short side if at all. When they take funerals, they almost invariably do so with dignity and sensitivity. (About three-quarters of all Scottish funerals are conducted by the Kirk's ministers.) Perhaps the best way of defining the rôle of the ministers is to say that they are local 'bishops'. Indeed in ecumenical arguments (i.e. those involving schemes for Christian unity) many a Presbyterian will still maintain that the reason his Church does not require new bishops is because it already has them within a Presbyterian council system which includes a much stronger democratic element than in many Churches.

But how did Scotland acquire such a distinctive national Church as, say, for example, the Church of England, south of the Border? Perhaps history does not solve the problems of the future, but it is needed to explain the present. And it is to the history of the Kirk that we turn in the next chapter.

How we came to be what we are

The history of the Christian Church for any country begins with Jesus Christ. The first news of Him almost certainly came to what is now Scotland when it was on the fringe of the Roman Empire. The first identifiable example of the universal Church in Scotland (and therefore of the Scots Kirk) arrived with Ninian, a British saint, who lived around AD 400. Although mainly associated with Whithorn in Galloway, he probably brought Christianity to many of the Pictish people. Mungo, or Kentigern (d. AD 603), traditional patron saint of Glasgow, belonged to the Church which Ninian helped to establish among the Britons.

The next great saint in early Scottish history was Columba, or Columkille (AD 521-597) who came from Ireland to Iona in the sixth century. He is often wrongly credited with the foundation of the Church of Scotland but, nevertheless, he was a great man with much influence. His followers created a Celtic Church in Scotland similar to the one existing in Ireland. It had a strong monastic element.

This Church not only changed the lives of Scots (originally from Ireland), Picts and Britons, but also converted the Northumbrian Angles, whose kingdom and culture stretched across the present-day Border from the Forth to Yorkshire. Cuthbert and Aidan were among the saints of this Church.

Politics eventually led to the triumph in England of a later missionary tradition inspired from Western Europe and linked to Rome. Eventually Scotland, encouraged by Queen Margaret, wife of King Malcolm Canmore, also became part of the same Church tradition, with its emphasis on Latin rather than Celtic ways. (Although sometimes called Saint Margaret of Scotland, Queen Margaret, d. 1093, was English by birth and Scots by marriage.) In the following centuries, the Scottish Church showed some of the best and the worst aspects of the

mediæval Church, with its mixture of artistic achievement, piety, corruption and superstition.

The Scottish Church built superb cathedrals, notably in Glasgow. However, in Orkney, Kirkwall also acquired a worthy cathedral, but at that time it was part of the Scandinavian Church. Scotland also possessed great Border abbeys which were ravaged during the Anglo-Scottish wars before the Reformation. They never recovered. Scotland had two other great ecclesiastical buildings in Elgin and St Andrews, which fell into ruin after the Reformation, more by neglect than determined destruction. Compared with England, there were relatively few country parish churches of distinction, except in parts of Lothian and Fife.

The Reformation in Scotland was both an intellectual and a radical popular movement although the Gaelic-speaking Highlands were not then greatly involved. It had relatively few martyrs, but among the few were the saintly Patrick Hamilton and George Wishart. The Reformation did, however, possess an outstanding leader and preacher in John Knox (1514-1572), a brilliant, warm-hearted, but single-minded man. His clash with the ambitious, attractive, but devious Mary, Queen of Scots (1542-1587), a devout Roman Catholic, committed to the French alliance and seeking the English throne, is a dramatic episode in Scottish history. There was also a new wave of Protestant leaders including such men as Andrew Melville and Robert Bruce. They, as much as Calvin's friend and disciple Knox, created the Presbyterian system of church government (sometimes they get credited with a 'second reformation') and applied Reformation Calvinist theology in ways which set their mark on the Scottish national character.

But the Calvinists did not have things all their own way, especially when James VI (and I of England, 1566-1625) and his son Charles I (1600-1649) wanted to keep the Kirk under royal control. Charles provoked a Scottish National Covenant of

Mary, Queen of Scots

James VI and I

protest; one of several covenants or solemn associations. This was one of the great national moments and movements of Scottish history.

After the complications of the English and Scottish civil wars, the tables were turned at the restoration of Charles II (1630-1685). He broke his promises to the Covenanters (the supporters of the National Covenant) who were subsequently persecuted and

often martyred at that time, particularly in Galloway and the south-west of Scotland. The Stuart Kings tried to rule the Church by imposing bishops on it (one of whom, Leighton of Dunblane, was to build up an enduring Christian reputation) but their plans collapsed in the English Revolution of 1688 which brought William of Orange to the throne. Although the Stuart Pretenders (by now Roman Catholics) still exploited

John Knox 1514-72

Roland Portchmouth

Scotland's internal divisions of Highlanders and Lowlanders, the long argument within the Kirk, about whether to have pure Presbyterianism or a modified Episcopal system, was settled in 1690. Since then the national Church has been Presbyterian in its structure.

After that settlement, which made the Scots Church permanently Presbyterian, two groups remained obviously outside; the Roman Catholics, who retained the loyalty of parts of the Highlands and Islands; and the Episcopalians, the supporters of the bishops. Both linked most of their hopes to the exiled Stuarts and were held suspect for political reasons during and after the Jacobite rebellions of 1715 and 1745, when the Church of Scotland took the Hanoverian side (as even some Highland clans did) against the Old Pretender and his son, the so-called Bonnie Prince Charlie (1720-1788). The romantic legends only flourished once there was no chance of getting the Stuarts back into power. The Highlanders who followed the Pretender deserved a better cause.

But even some groups of Presbyterians found themselves outside the structure of the national Church. At first only some extreme Covenanters stood out. Later, various groups broke away from the Church of Scotland, i.e. seceded, to try to keep the Church purer (as they saw it) and especially to keep it clear of what they considered to be a false compromise with the State which, since the Parliamentary Union with England in 1707, was British and not just Scottish. This issue of State control was to tear Scots Presbyterianism apart in the next century. The 1707 Union included a guarantee that the Scots Church would be Presbyterian. But the Scots lairds and the London Parliament combined were sometimes at odds with the ideas of the Scots congregations. While the Kirk was ruled by groups called the 'Moderates' (often men of great learning and culture), the conflict produced no more than a few secessions. But with the Evangelical revival, the quarrels became more frequent, and Scots judges gave decisions which seemed to suggest that the State could regulate the spiritual affairs of the Church. The London Government and most of the Scots aristocracy agreed with the judges and wanted the more co-operative Moderates to run the Kirk. But many ministers, elders and congregations passionately supported the other side. They were backed by a minority of the gentry and

Thomas Chalmers 1780-1847

probably a majority of the growing commercial middle class.

The outcome, delayed until 1843, was a major split in the Church of Scotland. It is known as the Disruption. About a third of the Church membership left its kirks and manses, starting literally with an exodus from the General Assembly. The participants represented at least half, perhaps more, of the most deeply committed people of the Kirk. Led by the greatest Scotsman of the age, Thomas Chalmers, they created a free Church, soon to be known as the Free Kirk. But it was a bitter quarrel, as family quarrels so often are. It was also another great and noble moment in Scottish history.

Eventually, in 1900, the main part of the Free Kirk linked up with the main body of the earlier seceders, who by now were known as United Presbyterians. As the old quarrel faded, a formula emerged by which the Kirk could keep its national standing without State control, and in 1929, what had become the United Free Church, was

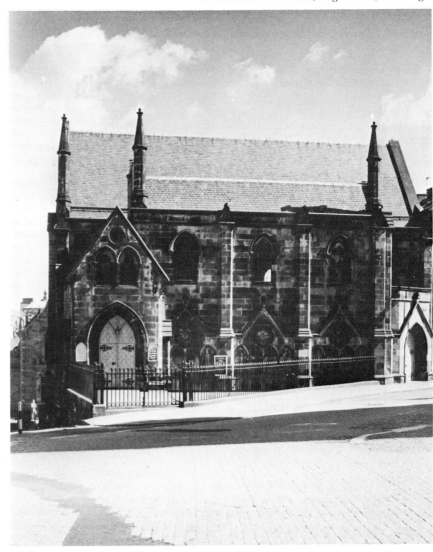

St Columba's Free Kirk, High Street, Edinburgh

reunited with the established Church of Scotland.

Thus it came about that the vast majority of Scots Presbyterians were reunited in 1929 and have stayed united ever since. Eventually even a remnant of original Seceders were gathered in. However, several other small Presbyterian Churches (like one United Free group) remained outside. The most important of these non-participants is probably the Free Church, or 'Wee Frees', who kept out of the 1900 union. Small in number, but intense in commitment, they are still largely Highland, conservative in theology and inclined to regard the Church of Scotland as far too liberal. They think it is not true enough to its Reformed Calvinist tradition and beliefs. They regard the Church of Scotland as a rather large black sheep of the same Presbyterian family, yet still believe in the idea of a national, Reformed Kirk.

There were also other trends and events in the 19th century which were to affect the religious life of Scotland in the next century. One was the vast Scots emigration which made many

Reformed Churches elsewhere in the English-speaking world very Scottish in character. Another was the Scots rôle in the missionary movement, which also gave the Kirk an international outlook and overseas connections.

Back home there was, for a time, an upper-class drift away from the Kirk, which revived and reshaped what remained of native Scots Episcopalianism. It was influenced both by the Oxford Movement and by 'public-school' religion (in the English sense). Its adherents did not (and do not) like being conveniently labelled the 'English Church', but their 19th century history was inextricably linked to the public-school kind of anglicisation. They are part of the Anglican Communion but are not always keen to be called Anglicans, which sounds too English for some of them.

Far more numerically significant was the vast Irish immigration into the West of Scotland, and even to Edinburgh and Dundee, during the Industrial Revolution. Some were Ulster Protestants, but most were Roman Catholics. This Irish immigration meant the creation of a relatively large Roman Catholic Church in Scotland (although for a long time the top jobs among Scots Catholics were still mostly reserved for the small minority of Highland and other Scots, rather than the Irish, who had remained Romanist). This explains why, in the 20th century, the Roman Church has emerged (especially in the industrial West of Scotland) as the only other really large Church in Scotland apart from the Kirk. Its exact size is a matter for some statistical argument, as the 'Catholic population' of about 820 000 out of 5 000 000 Scots is not comparable with most Protestant statistics (although the World Council of Churches uses an approximate figure of two million to estimate the Church of Scotland's 'community' population).

But of course the most important trend from the early 19th century onwards has been the drift away from any organised Church life by a large part of the Scots population, and, perhaps now, even of the largely Irish-descended Scots Roman Catholic community. The decline started in the cities and industrial areas but, long before the First World War, it was beginning to affect the countryside too. Among all the changes, however, the Kirk remains *the* Scottish Church; the Church which is attended regularly by some people, only occasionally by others. And there are others still who complacently stay away but expect the Church to be there when they want it. But it is our Church, truly our Church if we are an active part of it; our Church, in a way, even if we are not. It is the Church about which we have to know something if we are to understand Scots history and appreciate the character of this country and its people.

What we believe

It is in the hearts of its people rather than in any statement of faith that the beliefs of the Church of Scotland are best found. As the revivalist chorus says of Jesus Christ, 'You ask me how I know He lives . . . He lives within my heart'. That life is made possible by the Bible, the Word of God. It is the great channel of Christian communication and revelation. It is the Church of Scotland's 'supreme rule' of life and faith, and its primary standard. Different interpretations of the Bible or different ways of approaching it do not affect that supremacy.

But like other parts of the universal Church, the Kirk has felt a need for statements of the faith. That is why it often uses the ancient statements of faith called creeds, which are attempts to define the beliefs that Christians hold in common. The Kirk does so because it believes that the doctrines in them are derived from the Bible. Also derived from the Bible is the confession, or statement of faith which, for more than 300 years, has been the Kirk's principal 'subordinate standard'. It is not a Scottish document, although Scots went to England to take a share in drawing up this 'Westminster Confession'. Inevitably it reveals many indications of the times in which it was compiled and it contains matters which were then thought to demand special definition. But it has long been possible for the ministers and elders who assent to it, as containing the fundamental doctrines of Christian faith, to retain liberty of conscience and interpretation on matters not affecting the fundamental 'substance of the faith'.

In 1984, a proposal was discussed to alter this form of words and to add three new 'principal subordinate standards' to the Westminster Confession; the ancient Nicene and Apostles' Creeds and the Scots Confession of 1560 (the year of the Reformation of the national Church). This, sometimes called John Knox's Confession, was the great manifesto of the Scots reformers. But the new plan failed to win support from the majority of Presbyteries.

What the 'substance of the faith' is has been notoriously difficult to define. However, since its reunion in 1929, the Kirk has also possessed a constitution which goes a long way to providing a short statement of how our Church perceives the basic beliefs of its faith. Its official name is the Declaratory Articles but it takes the form of a written constitution.

The following are the propositions most clearly emerging from these Articles. (The full text is most easily found in Cox's *Practice and Procedure in the Church of Scotland*):

The Kirk is part of the universal or catholic worldwide Church. It is a Trinitarian Church; i.e. it sees God as Father, Son and Holy Spirit: three aspects of the one God.

It believes in God as Father and Creator, 'in whom are all things'.

It believes that Jesus was (and is) His 'eternal Son, made man for our Salvation'. In other words Jesus was not just a very good man who taught the right things, He was, and is, someone and something utterly special.

It believes that He, who died and rose again, is Head of the Church; the only Head of the Church.

And it believes that Christians are also promised renewal and guidance from the Holy Spirit.

The same basic document affirms the Protestant character of the Kirk ('the Church of Scotland adheres to the Scottish Reformation') and affirms the Bible as its 'supreme rule' of faith and life. It also commits the Church of Scotland to worldwide mission.

But no document, either a historic creed or a modern constitution, can really sum up a living faith. The Bible is not a series of definitions, but a series of inspired experiences through which God Himself is revealed. And He is further revealed in the life and faith of the people of the Church, especially in their discovery of the presence of Jesus, not just in their attempt to follow His teaching.

Not all members of the Kirk express their belief in Christian doctrines in the same way or in the same words. Some can find it hard to put their belief into words. But all believe (unless they have lapsed from the reality of membership) in God as Father and Creator. They also believe in the available power of the Holy Spirit and in Jesus Christ who is so special that He must be called God's only begotten Son.

What else is at the heart of faith in our Church? Most members of the Kirk would probably list these beliefs, among others: the inspiration of the Bible; the divine commission to the Church; the forgiveness of sins through Jesus (and only through Jesus); and what the creed calls the 'life everlasting', a belief that the death of the human body is not the end of our personality. But faith is essentially an experience of God, not an attempt to define Him. It is both a very personal affair, and, in the Church, something that is strengthened by sharing.

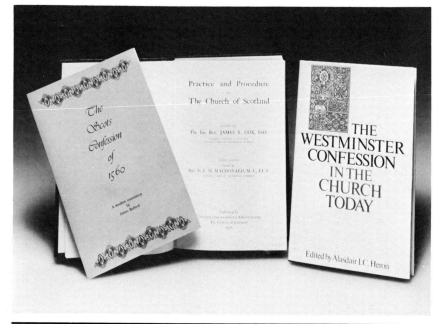

Our Church's worship

The pattern of worship in the Church of Scotland varies quite widely. Sometimes this is a reflection of the taste and style of the minister, who is responsible for the conduct of worship. Some ministers are sensitive, however, to the needs and wishes of their congregations. This can reflect the very diverse situations of congregations: for example, large or small, city or country, English or Gaelic-speaking, prosperous or poor. Experienced ministers consult their elders and members about worship, particularly about changes in the pattern more familiar to their church. Ministers also need to maintain a close and happy relationship with the chief musician who is professionally responsible for leading the congregation's praise.

There is a distinctive pattern of Scots Presbyterian worship, despite variations. These variations can range from cathedral-type worship (with elaborate music and prayers with congregational responses) to Gospel-type choruses with hand-clapping and perhaps an invitation to sing the chorus again more loudly! But most Scots churches are found somewhere in the broad area between these extremes of style. The Presbyterian pattern is not an unchanging one. In the past, sermons and prayers were much longer than they usually are today, and there were no hymns, only metrical psalms and sung paraphrases of parts of the Bible. In the 19th century, there were arguments about the introduction of organs. Today most congregations have organs, although church music can also be played on instruments ranging from guitars to even a string orchestra on special occasions.

The usual pattern of worship incorporates an opening hymn or, more likely, a metrical psalm or paraphrase. Often this is preceded by a brief call to worship: for example, 'This is the day of the Lord's victory; let us be happy, let us celebrate.' *(Psalm 118:24)* although older worshippers will find the Authorised Version more familiar: 'This is the day *which* the Lord hath made; we will rejoice and be glad in it'.

After the opening psalm or hymn, almost invariably comes a prayer or a series of prayers. Some ministers use set patterns of prayer while others try to avoid them. (We do not have prayer-books in our congregations.) The prayer usually includes a kind of general confession and thanksgiving, and probably ends with everyone saying together the words of the Lord's Prayer: 'Our Father . . .'. The version we use tends to be the one which refers to our 'debts' (from Matthew's Gospel in the Authorised or King James Version of the Bible) rather than the one with 'trespasses', although both are used in the Kirk.

Then a Bible reading follows. Often, but not always, there will be a second reading later. There is not necessarily a set pattern of Old and New Testament lessons. If the minister has an assistant or a student attached to his church, he or she may take a prayer. In some churches, the elders usually read the Bible passages, which may be from the Authorised translation, or from another version. Both the New English Bible and the Good News Bible are widely used.

After the next hymn many ministers give a children's address. But at this point in the service there could be a Baptism. After another hymn might come the 'collection' or the 'offering'. Ministers often think that the difference in the word itself reflects an important difference in attitudes. Some churches make their collection towards the end of the service, and a few cling to the old tradition of a plate at the door.

Churches with a strong choir (and even some with a weak one) may then have an anthem. Then after another hymn, comes the sermon. Nowadays, it may last for 15 minutes or perhaps as few as ten. Only in a few churches does it last much longer than 20 minutes. The sermon is meant to be the preaching of the Word, based on the Word of God, the Bible, although not necessarily from a particular text. It ought to stir, worry, stimulate and encourage the congregation. Often it does. To most Presbyterians, and in most Reformed worship, it is the high

point of the service. There follows, in most churches, a final hymn and the benediction or blessing. But some ministers might place an intercessory prayer (for particular needs and people) after the sermon although it is more common to include it earlier.

This general pattern is that of the main Sunday morning service, probably at 11.00 am. Some churches may also conduct less formal evening or weekday services. (Many traditional-type evening services were discontinued when television became almost universal.) Some busy churches hold two services on Sunday mornings, the first of them perhaps at 9.30 am, whereas small country churches may hold their services at unusual times so that the minister can arrange to take them in several different locations each Sunday.

Those of you from other branches of the Christian Church may be struck not by what this summary includes, but by what it omits: i.e. the form of worship that Christians variously call The Lord's Supper, Communion, Eucharist, or The Mass. The normal pattern of Scots Presbyterian worship does not hold Communion at the main

Sunday service, except on very special occasions. Instead it makes Communion a festival (perhaps quarterly) or includes it as a less formal addition to perhaps one service a month. Weekly Communion services do exist, however, but only in a minority of churches.

Some Scots Presbyterians favour more frequent Communion. Others regard their customary practice as the one which suits them best; the one which enhances the wonder of the occasion, just as Easter or Christmas services do. The Lord's Supper and Baptism (the other 'Gospel' sacrament) will be discussed later to show how they fit into our Church's way of doing things.

Incidentally, as Presbyterians we do not think that we have the monopoly on Christian wisdom in worship. We enjoy the experience of alternative customs at home and abroad. But our own ways are dear to us. We are at ease with them and have many happy memories and wonderful experiences associated with them. Although they change more than many people realise, they also include powerful and valuable elements of continuity and tradition.

Festivals, weddings and funerals

Every Christian service ought to be a festival. The greatest Christian festival should be the regular Sunday 'Lord's Day', the first day of the week. Sunday services should be celebrations. However, Calvinists are not people of the calendar, but of the Word. At times (quite often in Scotland) they have protested against the corruptions and diversions which can occur when worship becomes a routine. Saints' days and calendar celebrations can intrude upon the wonder that Christians ought to feel every day, and which they celebrate every Sunday.

Of course Calvinists are fallible too. They can be victims of routine. The old Scots Sabbath (i.e. Sunday, as defined by the Hebrew name for Saturday) had many merits. It was a day of much-needed rest. But it could become not only too solemn but too bleak, especially for those only nominally committed to the faith. To see its virtues and problems today, you only have to go to the Isle of Lewis, for example, where the inhabitants still respect the old Scots Sabbath.

Our Church nowadays tries to strike a balance in its style of worship and allows a wider discretion among congregations and ministers. In some places much more is made of 'the Christian year' than in others. For example, Whitsun (or Pentecost: the commemoration of the way in which the disciples were inspired by the Holy Spirit seven weeks after Easter) is probably a time of intense and joyful celebration only for a minority in the Scottish Church. Furthermore, there was even a time when Presbyterian Scotland did not make much of Christmas. Most of us would now say that that was a mistake. But at least it did help to ensure that Scots who wanted to make fools of themselves did so during the secular New Year festival, thus avoiding the modern problem of keeping Christmas in a not very Christian style. Today there is a general, almost universal, celebration of Christmas and Easter in our Church. Perhaps Christmas is the more popular festival. Theologically that may be unsound, but it partly reflects the social and even the economic context in which the Church lives and serves. Almost everybody (Scrooges excepted) wants to enjoy some kind of Christmas. We almost all have happy childhood memories of it. The Christmas festival of light amid the darkness is perhaps more readily shared than the festival of resurrection, which as a seasonal occasion probably finds the Mediterranean climate more congenial than the Northern European one, which can be a damp, cold setting for the festival of new life.

Of course, it would be an exaggeration to say that all the kirks are full at Christmas and half-empty at Easter, but the exaggeration points towards the truth. But despite all its faults, the modern Christmas remains a point of contact between Christ and those who are usually unconcerned as well as uncommitted. One sign of this is the steady increase in the number of Presbyterian midnight services, held as Christmas Eve turns into Christmas Day, although critics sometimes complain that on these occasions the church may 'smell of beer and bad theology'. In fact the increase in attendance was steady until some congregations began to have second thoughts after trouble with unsteady visitors who had probably been taking something a bit stronger than beer! Some churches are, as a result, trying 8.00 pm Christmas Eve services. Most midnight services, however, are becoming well-established, and are now almost as much a part of the modern Presbyterian Christmas as the children's party. Christmas Day services are also held, when a large part of the attendance is of families with young children.

Easter means even more to many people (perhaps it should to all Christians) but it is still largely neglected by the world outwith the Church, except as a Spring holiday. Holy Week services are common but far from universal, and Good Friday is not yet a general public holiday in Scotland. And although many churches have a Communion

service on Easter Sunday, the occasion is not quite the test of continuing commitment that it appears to be in England. Indeed in most kirks, the rôle of Easter Sunday, the 'high holy day and festival', is still largely taken by the statutory Communion services which have a higher than

average attendance and an intensity both in preaching the Word and responding to it that remains distinct from that of an 'ordinary' Sunday. Minister and congregation, in different ways, can emerge exhilarated but exhausted.

Even in congregations which do not make much of the 'Christian Year', there is inevitably a kind of rhythm to the seasons, not just Christmas and Easter and the great Communions, but Harvest Thanksgiving and Remembrance Sunday as well; and also that noticeable quickening of congregational activity once most people's summer holidays are over. Then the Sunday school resumes. The youth and other organisations get going again: the Woman's Guild, the badminton, the country dancing and, in many congregations, regular Bible study and prayer meetings.

For most people, however, the great festivals they associate with their local church are not necessarily those of 'the Christian Year', but those of their own lives and those of their family's. Baptism (see separate chapter) is a

A marriage ceremony

sacrament but it is also usually a great family festival. Weddings are festivals the world over. And funerals may be defined as festivals too; solemn perhaps, but in a respectful and Christian manner (especially after a long life and peaceful end) they can be joyful occasions.

Just under 60 per cent of all Scots weddings are now held in church; a clear majority of those in the Church of Scotland. But the proportion of civil marriages has been rising, and many people (although perhaps fewer than the number in England) see the choice not so much as between a religious and secular ceremony, but between a 'big wedding', (i.e. in church) and a small or quiet one. In fact, a religious wedding in Scotland can be as quiet an affair as the participants care to make it; the licence to conduct religious marriages in Scotland is not concerned with place of worship or registry, but with persons, notably the minister. But most church weddings, whether big or small, are family festivals and, in their own way, Christian festivals too. Generally they are held in the bride's church, although this varies according to circumstances and inclinations.

There are two points about weddings in our Church which are worth making at this stage. The first is that the Church of Scotland takes a very flexible Christian view about 'mixed' marriages; a term which, in Scotland, generally means a marriage between a Protestant and a Roman Catholic. There has been some easing of the hard line taken by the Roman Catholic Church, but this still remains a sensitive and, at times, difficult area, mainly because of the Roman pressure to have children of such marriages brought up as Catholics. And although Presbyterians and other Protestants are anxious that children in this situation should be brought up as Christians, they also want to be true to their own Christian conscience.

The second point is that the Kirk gives a wide discretion to its ministers on the remarriage of divorced people. This has spared our Church the recent painful experience of the Church of England in trying to be firm in doctrine, yet charitable to people in pastoral need. Ministers use this discretion in different ways, but most now find that the desire for a second marriage in church generally arises when one, or both, of the partners feels deeply about the religious significance of marriage. There are usually about 1200 marriages a year in our Church involving divorced people; about eight per cent of all the Kirk's weddings.

Funerals (which in urban areas now generally involve cremations and not burials) are also festivals in their own way and are inevitably family occasions. For many families with no formal church connections, funerals are now the main occasion on which they come into close contact with a minister, usually the minister of the parish where they live. Very often now this contact does not even occur in church, for the service may be held in a crematorium chapel.

The funeral service remains perhaps the most important of pastoral duties and pastoral opportunities. This is especially true if, as is often the case, the minister does not merely take the service, but visits the bereaved family before and afterwards. An experienced minister knows how much funerals matter. To handle a funeral badly is far more serious than to be late for a wedding or to get the names of the babies mixed up at a christening!

Indeed, it is remarkable how rarely complaints about ministers (inevitably there are a few – usually about pastoral visiting) are concerned with funerals. In this secularised age, despite its decline in church membership and attendance, the dignity and sensitivity with which Scots funerals are handled are probably among the main reasons why Scots ministers retain a far wider and deeper respect than the general statistics of the Kirk, or even the lukewarm reception of some sermons, would suggest. It is not easy for a minister to handle a funeral if he knows the bereaved family only slightly, or not at all. But the work is still essential, and is usually well-done and well-received. For the funeral is the church service in which, sooner or later, almost every Scot will decide, in advance of course, to take part.

The Sacraments

To many people a 'sacrament' is a name for any religious rite. Christians, however, have to be more precise. Our Church believes and teaches that there are two sacraments: Baptism and the Lord's Supper (which in Scotland is commonly called Communion). A sacrament is a sign, although it may also involve a ceremony. The people of the Church of Scotland believe that these two signs of God's goodness to His people strengthen and increase their faith and help make them feel part of a Christian family. Sometimes the sacraments are also described as 'seals', fastening God's people to Him and to each other.

Our Church believes that there are two sacraments because it finds the evidence and command for them in the New Testament: that is, in the teaching of Jesus himself. Some groups of Christians do not have sacraments at all. Larger groups have more numerous rites which they call sacraments. But Reformed Christians find no biblical reason for doing so. For example, we cherish Christian marriage and believe it involves promises to God as well as between the partners. We do not, however, see it as a sacrament. Nor do we regard such practices, procedures or ceremonies as Confession, Extreme Unction (the 'Last Rites'), Confirmation and Ordination as sacraments. In this we take the general view of Protestant Christians.

Only the two Gospel 'sacraments' seem to us to merit this solemn title and to justify the theological inquiry which, for centuries, Christians have devoted to their meaning and practice. Baptism and the Lord's Supper we see as signs in two ways: we try to make a solemn public demonstration which is a sign of what Christ did for us and that we belong to Him, but we also believe that the outward sign is combined with an inward grace; the outward sign is a visible symbol of something deep which is easier to sense than to define lucidly.

Baptism

Baptism is both a ceremony of admission and a sacrament. In the Church of Scotland over 90 per cent of those who are admitted to the Christian Church in this way are too young to understand what is happening. We practise what is called 'infant baptism', not only because it is a tradition of our Church (and most of the Churches of other Christians) but because we find it consistent with New Testament evidence.

In the ceremony of Baptism, the parents (or sometimes just one parent) take vows to bring up the child in the Christian family. Thus the Baptismal ceremony, usually contained in a main morning service, is an occasion of dedication and thanksgiving as well as part of a happy family occasion. About one third of the children born in Scotland these days are baptised in the Church of Scotland as infants, usually when about two or three months old.

In our Church we do not have official 'godparents', although the name is sometimes applied to close family friends, especially the woman-friend or relative

Baptism in Scotland: John Philips   *Aberdeen Art Gallery and Museums*

who, walking next to the parents, carries the baby into church. However, this has no theological significance, for the vows are taken by the parents alone.

Between five and ten per cent of Church of Scotland Baptisms are of adults. In these cases the person who is to be baptised takes his or her own vows, and the service may well be a small, private one. Often these adult Baptisms are preludes to the individual concerned 'joining the Church' or being 'confirmed'. The latter word, perhaps more familiar in the English Church, is used by many Scots congregations to denote the admission of adults as communicant or 'full' members of the Church. Perhaps in the future the proportion of adult Baptisms will increase. People who are drawn to the Christian faith in their adult life may find that they have never been baptised. This is not unusual.

We believe that Baptism can only be given once to any person. Our Church in the past did not rebaptise people who came into it from other Christian denominations. But now most Churches recognise one another's Baptism. This once-only rule can create problems (some of which have reached the stage of General Assembly argument) for people who have been baptised in childhood, but who have had a religious experience as adults which seems to them to demand some visible sign of their conversion. Possibly we need a more personal opportunity for dedication than the service of Admission or Confirmation often provides.

However, our Church believes that Baptism is so solemn and sacramental an act that it would be wrong to repeat it for any person. Sometimes one hears of a child, for example, being baptised in a Norwegian or German church and then a Scots one. Any competent theologian could probably argue that these two services really added up to one Baptism, even if the water were sprinkled twice!

Our Church rejects the superstitious fears that sometimes accompany Baptism, or those which add to the grief over the death of an unbaptised person: for example, a very young child. We think that it is a mistake for Christians to neglect Baptism, but we do not think that salvation depends upon it. Nor do we think that it is anyone's passport to Heaven!

The Lord's Supper

If anyone thinks that The Lord's Supper is an extremely formal name for Communion, then they should remember that it is a solemn re-enactment of the Last Supper:

'. . . the Lord Jesus, on the night he was betrayed, took a piece of bread, gave thanks to God, broke it, and said, "This is my body, which is for you. Do this in memory of me". In the same way, after the supper he took the cup and said, "This cup is God's new covenant, sealed with my blood. Whenever you drink it, do so in memory of me." ' *(I Corinthians 11:23-25).*

These are Paul's words to the Corinthians, in the Good News version of the Bible. Paul's words, and what is said in the Gospels, explain why we do what we do. No-one should think, because we in our Church break

Covenanter's Communion: George Harvey   *National Gallery of Scotland, Edinburgh*

the bread and drink the wine relatively infrequently, that we set a lesser value on the Lord's Supper (or Communion) than some other Churches. Far from it. One of the problems concerning frequent Communion, despite Calvin being in favour of it, is the need for the Word to be preached in a way that matches the great occasion. We believe that a proper Communion sermon should leave a minister with nothing more that needs to be said and very little strength with which to say it.

Many Churches now hold monthly Communions and extra Communion on special or seasonal occasions. But, as we have seen, in almost all Scots Presbyterian Churches, there still are appointed Communion Sundays (four a year perhaps) which themselves become festivals. That is when the Church is fullest, when the congregation is most attentive and when the minister faces the greatest challenge and opportunity.

The celebration of Communion usually follows the sermon. On the Table (we never speak of 'altars') the bread and the wine-cups are spread. The Bible's 'warrant' is read, followed by prayer. The crucial words are repeated. The first bread is broken and the cup is raised before the people who are to share it: 'Let all drink from it'. In our Church, it is unusual for people to come forward to receive the bread and wine, although that style of ceremony is to be found in some places. Ideally the bread and wine of the Communion should be served to the people at specially prepared tables. Modern church architecture and the layout of the pews mean that the sharing and serving is carried out by the elders, who have been gathered around the Table. They take the bread and then the wine among the people, serving them and asking them to pass the plate and cup on so that they can serve each other. This is usually done in a reverent silence. It is unusual for a choir to sing or for the organ to play during this time. This is in marked contrast to the presence of a string orchestra, playing Bach perhaps, while German Lutherans share the sacrament at one of their great festivals (such as the service at Worms commemorating the 500th birthday of Martin Luther).

We do not have precisely set forms of Communion and there are variations in our practice on many aspects. Some ministers even make a point of using parts of the traditional structure of the Communion service of other churches: for example, the *Agnus Dei* ('Lamb of God prayer'). Many choose not to. But of course, the words about the bread and wine, which come directly from the Bible, are those of the universal Church. However, Communion is not merely an impressive ceremony contrived by human ingenuity. It is part of God's provision for us, commended by God through the words of Jesus Christ and 'The Word'.

In modern times our Communion services have also included an invitation which would be a good thing to hear at every Christian Communion service. For the minister presiding at the Table to 'celebrate Communion' is not a very Presbyterian concept. All our congregation are there to celebrate. Furthermore, the minister invites all present who are members of other parts of the Christian Church, to join in the taking of the bread and wine. For the Table is the Lord's, and not the Church's. He may also remind everyone present that, although the Lord's Table is a place where they must think searchingly about their lives, the emphasis ought to be on God's grace and goodness, not on their own sinfulness. This is certainly the modern Presbyterian outlook, although there are still traces of the times when the emphasis was on trying to warn the unworthy of the dangers of taking the elements lightly.

But the occasion also has to embody the joyful celebration of Christ's presence among his people and provide a living memorial to His sacrifice for us; the one marvellous, unrepeatable sacrifice. This is what we share in the sacrament of the Lord's Supper, often referred to in the speech of Scots people as 'The Sacrament'.

Communion Table with Common Cups and bread   *Baptismal font and ewer*

Roland Portchmouth

The Church's music

It is quite wrong to dismiss Scotland as an unmusical country. Modern Scotland has established itself as a significant place for composers, performers and responsive audiences. It is also the setting for a great deal of amateur skill and enthusiasm, with a large proportion of its voluntary and semi-professional musicians belonging to the Church and serving it, or rather serving God through it.

We have nothing in our musical tradition as sublime as the great German Protestant Church musician J S Bach and his gifted relatives: but who has? The Protestant biblical emphasis of our Church has never been married to great music as it was in, for example, Bach's versions of Our Lord's Passion, or Brahms's *German Requiem*. But we did join the English in making Handel an honorary Briton, and most of our church choir members are thoroughly familiar with his *Messiah*.

What we do possess, in a distinctively Scottish way, is the tradition whereby the whole congregation should sing to the Lord a joyful song. Sometimes

the tradition has been allowed to fall into a rut and sometimes the sense of joy has been lost. But at its best, Scotland has retained this Protestant affirmation in music (as the evangelical John and Charles Wesley did although in a different style) and supplied a modest, but worthwhile, contribution to the common heritage of Western Christendom.

For 300 years after the Reformation, the Kirk's congregational music consisted almost entirely of the metrical versions of the Psalms (which the Reformers wanted sung by the people to good tunes) and some 'passages of Scripture', paraphrased by being turned into verse. The literary and musical quality of this repertoire varied, although its core continued to be the sublime hymn-book of ancient Israel, revived and developed by the Calvinist Reformation. The English Prayer

Book reflected the same love of the Psalms, but the Presbyterians managed to bring them closer to the people.

In the metrical Psalms and Paraphrases of the Kirk there are admittedly some poorer passages and some awful rhymes. However, there are others which are so well known as hymns throughout the English-speaking world, that they are not always recognised as metrical Psalms or Paraphrases. Among them are *The Lord's My Shepherd, O God of Bethel, I to the Hills,* and that marvellous victory hymn, *Now Israel may say*; some of whose metrical verses match, in their different forms, the quality of the superb prose of the Authorised Version of the Bible. Some of the great tunes are Scots, others are imports. Some even date back to Calvin's original enthusiasm for music. This inheritance is not one that sensitive Scots neglect. Nor are they keen to see the Psalms and Paraphrases just scattered throughout a hymn-book, which is the case in some editions of our modern hymnary. The best of the metrical Psalms have the same effect on our people's religious

The organ in St Stephen's Church, Edinburgh

life as Burns' lyrics have had on Scottish popular culture.

In the 19th century, Scotland's musical taste widened and deepened. This happened both inside and outside the Church. In the Kirk, there were arguments about organs; 'kists o' whistles' as they were disparagingly referred to by their critics. Hymns also became more popular, although the Free Kirk and Free Presbyterians still avoid both organs and hymns. But the main body of Scots Presbyterians took to hymns joyfully, and even to anthems, demanding a choir able to perform and willing to practise. The organist, playing more for love than money, became a recognised musical leader of the congregation, although a different kind of leadership and lasting influence came from the Moody and Sankey tradition of Evangelical hymns.

The Victorian Kirk gave as well as took: George Matheson's *O Love that wilt not let me go,* and several of the numerous hymns of Horatius Bonar, are good examples of this. These hymns, like the best of the metrical Psalms and Paraphrases, are part of the Scots Presbyterian contribution to international and inter-denominational Christianity. The Victorians wrote many good hymns. The best of these, like the best 18th century Wesleyan ones, have survived their time. But since then church music has run into the problems of differing styles and preferences. Revisers of hymn-books are tempted to try to impose their theological and musical tastes on others, and can be cavalier in their view of much-loved hymns like *What a Friend we have in Jesus.* There are also pressures from quite different quarters to modernise or popularise the church's music. Faced with such conflicting points of view, combined with the vast gaps of generational and musical taste, the Church has sometimes sought safety in standing still. People feel comfortable with that which is familiar, and relatively few of the new hymns in any style have yet become part of our folk-culture.

A good deal of experimentation continues modestly, but the best of the older Scots musical inheritance is likely to remain part of the Church's life. This tradition will probably co-exist quite happily with new hymns from Africa, Asia and Latin America. In the same way, the Scots themselves continue to accept and absorb a good deal of the musical influence from England, Ireland, Wales and the United States, as our hymn-books and other Gospel music have shown.

The languages of the Kirk and the Bible

English became the language of the Scots Reformation and afterwards generations of Scots were brought up on the Authorised (or King James) Version of the Bible. Its marvellous prose was probably pronounced by Scots in a way that made this change to English less of a dramatic step away from the language of the Lowland people (a 'broad' Scots akin to English) than we might think.

But many Scots then spoke Gaelic, a Celtic language; to them, what we now call broad Scots was the English tongue. Over the centuries Gaelic has receded, but it remains the first language of many Highlanders and Hebridean islanders, and one of its most cherished uses is as a language of worship. But it took the Kirk a while to learn to preach and teach in a way that reached the hearts of the Highland people.

Our Church is still a bilingual Church; not in its government and administration, which are in English, but in its worship. (Gaelic however, may be used in local church business but the minutes are kept in English.) It is inevitably a very uneven division.

Less than three per cent of Scots speak Gaelic and many of those who do, live in English-speaking communities. And there are far fewer Gaelic services in Glasgow and Edinburgh than there used to be. In parishes where the Church used to regard Gaelic as a 'desirable' language for its minister, the old language has often vanished from worship when only an English-speaking minister was available. There are many Gaels in the ministry, but not all of them want to work in the Highlands and Islands. A considerable number serve congregations where there is no chance for them to use their first language. This is a sign of how proficient (and often eloquent) virtually all Gaels now are in English as well as Gaelic but it makes it harder to ensure that every parish, where Gaelic might be useful, has a bilingual minister. In the Outer Hebrides and parts of the Highlands, mainland Gaelic is still an essential language for the minister. In Lewis, or even Skye, it remains the first language of worship, although the Church of Scotland there always draws a proportion of its members from 'exiled' Lowlanders and, because of that, it sometimes seems less Gaelic than the Free Kirk or Free Presbyterians. However, it is the Church of Scotland which provides most of the 'religious Gaelic' still in print, in the form of a monthly supplement to its national magazine, *Life and Work*.

The future depends on the Gaels themselves. There are attempts to revive and modernise the language, yet there are still signs of decline. Television gets some of the blame; so too do Gaelic-speaking parents who speak English in conversation with their children. And, in a congregation or community where there are people who speak only English, a combination of Gaelic politeness and bilingualism tends to help English become more dominant. Children in families where only one parent speaks Gaelic are not always encouraged to learn both languages.

Above: *A Cranmer (or Great) Bible of 1562*

Below: *A Cranmer (or Great) Bible of 1549*

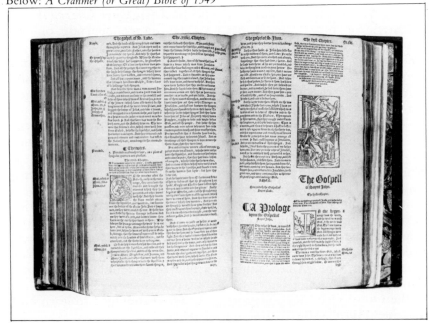

Both of these Bibles could have been in circulation in Scotland during the period of the Scottish Reformation

Gaelic has many fervent, even militant, advocates, but there is an anti-clerical streak in some of the more radical Gaelic revivalism. The Kirk (with the Church of Scotland perhaps accounted the most liberal of the Protestants) gets blamed for their restrictive, ultra-Calvinist attitude. There is also some evidence that young people in Gaelic-speaking areas incline towards English worship possibly because Gaelic services seem very traditional and formal. On the other hand, Gaelic-speaking ministers have been working on a translation of the Bible (or parts of it) into modern Gaelic and have sometimes been supported in their attempts to provide the Gaels with secular newspapers and magazines. Ministers often take the part of community leaders and have led attempts to use the language in local government on the Islands, which is probably one of the most successful means to help and revive the language. The fairest view perhaps is that Gaelic has retained a stronger place in the Church than it has done in most other areas of Highland

and Island life and, if it revives generally as a language of the community there, this will be reflected in the Church. If, however, it revives only as a 'hobby language', taken up by learners in the cities, this may not be reflected in church life to any great extent.

It might be asked if the Kirk ought to be 'tri-lingual', adding Scots to English and Gaelic. Some attempts have been made in churches to preach and pray in Scots, and in 1983 a very notable translation of the New Testament into Scots was published: *The New Testament in Scots,* translated by William Laughton Lorimer. This was a major addition to Scots literature and has been read in a number of churches, but in the present cultural climate it has had little impact on regular worship. As with Gaelic, the Church's use of the Scots language is likely to reflect what happens in the rest of society. For the moment, the main argument is whether worship should reflect the stately English of the Authorised Version of the Bible, or if it should become much more idiomatic. Although in 1946

the Kirk began the moves which led to the publication of the complete New English Bible in 1970, the present best-seller in congregations is the simpler Good News Bible, published in its 'British usage edition' in 1976. Some people even detect a movement back towards the

classic English of the Authorised Version, and new editions of the Bible exist which reflect this mood, showing only a minimum of change to the 17th century text.

However, the 1984 Scottish Church attendance census showed that for reading in

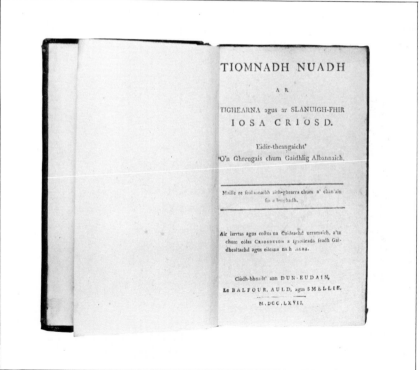

One of the first Gaelic Bibles, 1767

church, only a third of the Kirk's churches use the Authorised Version of the Bible, and slightly more the modern New English Bible. The Good News Bible (the simplest modern translation) was used in 29 per cent and the Revised Standard Version (closer to the Authorised Version) in 20 per cent. One can therefore say that just over half the Kirks use the Bible in its classic English form. (The numbers add up to more than 100 as some churches use more than one version.)

All this diversity of opinion is comparable to the arguments in the Church of England about the Prayer Book in its traditional and modern forms. The arguments are, however, less vital than the English ones, for the flexibility of Presbyterian worship means that those leading it, free from the constraint of set forms, can adapt the language of worship to their situation and their hearers. At their best, the ministers of the Kirk achieve this, even if talents in communication are unevenly shared among them. But inevitably the Kirk reflects some of the contemporary uncertainty about what makes 'good English', and whether there ought to be standards and conventions in its usage.

Some of our churches

2

A guided tour

A beautiful church does not give anyone a more direct line to God. Sometimes ornate and elaborate structures can even divert attention from the essential simplicity of truth and beauty. There is a strain of noble austerity in the Calvinist religion. What happens in the Kirk (and even more so, what happens in the hearts of those who go there) must matter more than the elaboration of the surroundings.

Yet Scotland has a noble and sometimes underestimated heritage of church buildings: pre-Reformation, post-Reformation, Classical Revival, Victorian and even 20th century. The great majority of these historic churches are Church of Scotland buildings. Some are illustrated here; chosen either because they are of outstanding importance as buildings, or because they say something distinctive about the character of the Scots Kirk. Rather more examples are sketched in words. Yet, inevitably, many valuable and historic buildings have had to go unmentioned.

Those of our churches illustrated or mentioned do, however, provide a taste of the Kirk's buildings. They are visible symbols of what the Kirk has meant in the history of Scotland and in the experience of Scots people and their glory and love of God. In most parts of Scotland, the parish church is a key part of the history of the parish.

There is no 'mother-church' in Scottish Presbyterianism to parallel Canterbury Cathedral's rôle in the Anglican Communion. In some ways, the nearest thing to it is Iona, the enchanted west-coast island, now in the hands of the National Trust for Scotland. Iona, where St Columba settled, a generation before Augustine reached Canterbury, is not the oldest Christian site in Scotland, but it is a sacred one. *Iona Abbey* was a roofless ruin at the start of this

St Mary's Abbey, Iona

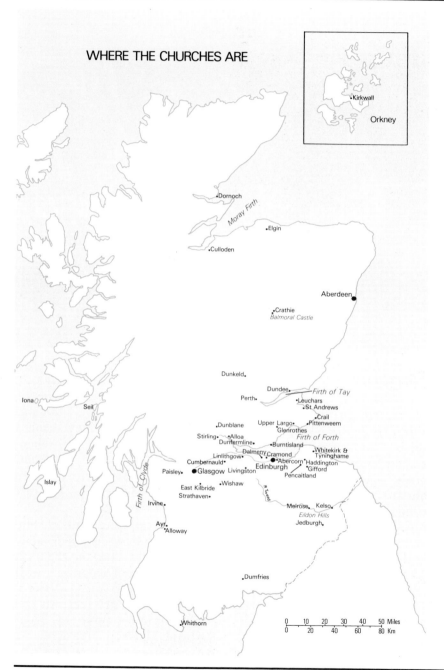

WHERE THE CHURCHES ARE

century but it is now restored. It was saved by two practical visionaries; the Duke of Argyll, at the turn of the century (who secured its future and its structure), and George MacLeod, founder of the Iona Community, which carried out the work of restoration from the 1930s.

Columba came to Iona from Ireland. From Iona, his sixth-century missionaries reached into Northern England and shaped the Northumbrian Christian culture which is well depicted by the Venerable Bede in his *History of the English Church and People*.

But even *Iona Abbey* (which is now in the hands of a board of trustees, not strictly speaking of the Kirk) yields precedence as a Christian site to *Whithorn* in Galloway, associated with the British saint, Ninian. He was the first great Christian to belong to what was later to become known as Scotland. More than a century before Columba, Ninian demonstrated how the Christian faith that began on one Roman frontier had spread to the opposite end of the Empire which was, by then, faltering.

St Andrew's Cathedral from St Regulus Tower

St Ninian's and St Columba's are popular names for Scots churches. But the mediæval choice of St Andrew as Scotland's patron saint (a pleasing association which survived even when it lost its dubious historical and theological basis at the Reformation) means that the Galilean fisherman, brother of Peter, has almost certainly more Presbyterian churches named after him than any other saint or apostle, ancient or modern. In any English-speaking country there are many St Andrew's churches to testify the influence of the Scots. But the most apparent link with Andrew is to be found at St Andrews in Fife. Once it was Scotland's ecclesiastical capital. Indeed, it possesses the country's oldest university. But now it is Mecca for the world's golfers. The old cathedral, like the castle where John Knox was imprisoned in a dungeon, has become a ruin. But the town has several stately kirks, including the 'town' church of *Holy Trinity,* and several fine buildings with university connections including *St Salvator's,* and the fine quadrangle of the Divinity school, *St Mary's College.*

Between St Andrews and Edinburgh, the 'kingdom of Fife' is possibly Scotland's richest area for interesting and historic parish churches, reflecting the church's place in farming, seafaring, fishing and industrial communities: for example, *Crail's* kirk dates from the 13th century; *Pittenweem's* church acquired its castle-like tower just after the Reformation; *Leuchars St Athernase* has a Norman church; *Upper Largo* has a 16th century chancel and tower, with a spire dating from 1623, whereas *Burntisland* (1592) has a distinctively Reformed style of church. The Reformers built and did not just adapt: they wanted churches to preach in, where people would hear the Word and respond, not just watch a mystery far above their heads at the east end of the Church.

At the opposite end of Fife from St Andrews is *Dunfermline Abbey,* rebuilt early in the 19th century on one of Scotland's most historic religious sites, where a Norman nave survives. In the church is the grave of King Robert Bruce, victor at Bannockburn.

St Columba's, Burntisland, Fife

The road from the Forth Bridge to Edinburgh is close to some ancient churches: for example, *Dalmeny, Abercorn,* and *Cramond,* which stands on the site where a Roman fort and supply base had once been built. Some of the archaeological potential cannot be excavated because it is directly underneath the kirk, but the main lines of the Roman base are marked out in the green surroundings. The present church building (the heart of it is 17th century) shows how a quiet country kirk can find itself becoming the central church of the new suburban community. Visible from the main road into Edinburgh is what was once *Cramond Free Church,* formed when the minister and elders all 'came out' on principle at the 1843 Disruption. Now it is *Davidson's Mains Parish Church,* with a neat modern extension for the increased congregation which Edinburgh's expansion has brought.

Cramond Kirk, Edinburgh

High Kirk (St Giles'), Edinburgh

Edinburgh's greatest city church is the *High Kirk* on the ridge of the Old Town: *St Giles' Cathedral,* with its noble crown steeple. It dates from the 15th century, but its time of greatness began when John Knox was the minister there. The Cathedral (the honorific title is commonly used) also contains the *Thistle Chapel* and the tombs of the great 17th century rivals, Montrose and Argyll; Covenanters of quite different kinds. Recently much-needed restoration work has been done to the Cathedral, a pleasant basement has been excavated, and the interior has been rearranged to give a feeling of community around the pulpit and Communion Table.

Nearby are *New College* and the Church's *Assembly Hall*; the great Victorian architectural complex (designed by Playfair) on the Mound, enriched from many viewpoints by the effect of the tall spire of the now disused *Tolbooth Church*. Down the Royal Mile from *St Giles',* almost at Holyroodhouse, is the delightful 17th century *Canongate (Holyroodhouse) Kirk,* notable in modern times for the long

Canongate (Holyroodhouse) Kirk, Edinburgh

St Mary's Episcopal Cathedral, Edinburgh

ministry of the wartime 'Radio Padre', Ronald Selby Wright.

Across in Edinburgh's New Town, the most spectacular church architecture belongs to the Episcopal *St Mary's Cathedral,* one of Britain's great Victorian Gothic buildings, designed by Sir Gilbert Scott, but there are several other important parish churches in the same area. *Palmerston Place,* for example, is a fine Parisian style Presbyterian church. *St Cuthbert's* at the west end of Princes Street Gardens evokes the spirit of Baroque, and *St George's West* (although its campanile catches the eye) really epitomises a church meant for a preaching ministry. In George Street, *St Andrew's and St George's* was the scene of the 1843 Disruption. It is an elegant, round church with a graceful spire. The *St George's* part of the name comes from the domed church, now West Register House, which is in Charlotte Square.

On the south side of central Edinburgh is one of the greatest churches of Scottish history: the post-Reformation (1612) *Greyfriars Kirk,* which now incorporates Edinburgh's Highland congregation. It is now world-famous due to the story of Greyfriars Bobby; the loyal dog that stood sentinel by its master's grave. More significant historically was the signing of the Great National Covenant of 1638 in *Greyfriars'* kirkyard. Later its kirkyard was used as a jail for Covenanters during their time of persecution.

Greyfriars' churchyard, Edinburgh

St Michael's, Linlithgow

The Cathedral (St Mungo's), Glasgow

Edinburgh is scarcely 40 minutes by train from Glasgow, with the rail traveller getting a splendid view of a mediæval church well worth a visit: *St Michael's,* Linlithgow. Its crown steeple collapsed in the 19th century and was replaced in the 1960s by Geoffrey Clarke's modern gilded variation, with more than a hint of the crown of thorns. Opinion was mixed at first, but the design has now probably found favour with most of the doubters.

Glasgow, arguably, has even more important examples of church architecture than Edinburgh, although redevelopment has thinned out the good and bad in its Victorian heritage. In fact, there has been such drastic redevelopment that it is hard to say precisely where some 19th century churches stood! One of the greatest church buildings in Scotland is probably *Glasgow Cathedral,* built on the site where the British saint, Mungo (or Kentigern) founded a church for the people of ancient Strathclyde. The building, a notable piece of Early English architecture, dates from the 12th century. Until the 19th century, Glasgow University was situated just down the hill, but the Victorians moved west, the old college site became a railway goods station, and the Royal Infirmary was built in a position that spoiled the setting of the cathedral. Modern redevelopment has made life difficult for the nearby and historic *Barony Church.* It is hard now to imagine the densely packed area in which the Auld Kirk Evangelical, Norman Macleod, had one of the great ministries in the Kirk's history, combining preaching, power and

social conscience. The Church has regretfully agreed to dissolve the congregation and dispose of the building.

The best of Glasgow's surviving Victoriana can be observed in such kirks as *Wellington Church,* which faces the main gate of Glasgow University. Built by the United Presbyterians, it shows the way in which this prosperous and progressive Church commissioned fine Victorian architecture without getting carried away (as the Auld Kirk and even the Free Kirk of the day were) by Gothic enthusiasm.

Indeed, *Wellington Church* looks more like a Greek temple. The 'square' church was better suited to the Reformed emphasis on preaching.

The United Presbyterians (UPs) encouraged the distinctive Victorian architect, 'Greek' Thomson (although his style was possibly more Byzantine or Egyptian), but much of his work has been lost. *St Vincent Street Church* still remains however, although it is not in the Kirk's charge. Another fine Victorian church, *Lansdowne,* with its slender spire rising above the River Kelvin, also has UP

origins. Other churches of the UP tradition (for example, in Kilmacolm and Milngavie) are surprisingly ornate. The UPs did not inhibit their late Victorian architects. The modern Kirk should not underestimate what this part of its ancestry contributed to it, aesthetically, theologically and intellectually.

Paisley, although a very independent place, is today in Greater Glasgow. It has several good churches embodying a great deal of social history in stone. The most important is the much restored *Paisley Abbey,* where a 15th century nave remains. The abbey was founded in 1163 as a Cluniac monastery by monks who originated from Cluny in France. The Cluniacs were revivalist Benedictines.

The characteristic church of the West of Scotland is not a nave, but a box. You can find this kind of church in Burns' country, many of them built during the time of the poet, not only in Ayrshire, but in Dumfries where Burns was buried in the kirkyard of *St Michael's*. Few are elaborate; almost all of these churches express architecturally the

St Michael's, Dumfries

Round Church, Bowmore, Islay

Presbyterian concept of doing things 'decently and in order'. Sometimes the decency becomes classical elegance, even as far afield as the Bowmore *Round Church* on the island of Islay. Such churches are only now beginning fully to be appreciated. The usual structure comprises an auditorium, which may have had a spire or tower added in days of greater prosperity (perhaps with a little help from influential 'moderate' ministers or aristocratic patrons). The churches of Eaglesham or Strathaven exemplify the dignity of this Scots style. Those with literary tastes, having seen the *Auld Kirk* at Ayr (Burns' home town), and the ruined old *Alloway Kirk* of Tam o' Shanter fame, could also take in *Dreghorn and Pearston Old Parish Church* in Irvine, which makes a veiled appearance in John Galt's classic gem of Scots Kirk life, *The Annals of the Parish*. Such kirks are best seen, of course, during Sunday worship and may well be closed at most other times.

In the days when these churches were built, weekday worship in Scotland meant family worship. Now, alas, many churches would like to keep their buildings open every day but have to beware of the wrong kind of souvenir hunters. However, a number of historic churches, especially in the cities, have volunteer guides: this means it is not only the few cathedrals which are open on weekdays.

But Scots religious history is not just a matter of buildings. The most moving religious monuments in south-west Scotland are quite literally commemorations, in particular to the persecuted 17th century Covenanters who gathered at their moorland conventicles. History is not only to be found in dour stone kirks, but on the open hill as well.

Perhaps the closest modern Presbyterian style to that of the Covenanters is to be found in the Highlands and even the Islands, although the influence of the Gaelic language and its traditions makes it hard to carry the comparison very far. Churches in the Highlands and Islands are generally very plain for economic as well as theological reasons, although there is a special

St Magnus Cathedral, Kirkwall, Orkney

historical interest in the group of Highland churches erected by the great engineer, Thomas Telford.

But there is one other island church to match and perhaps surpass *Iona Abbey,* not in the Gaelic isles of the Hebrides, but to the north in Orkney. There the culture and tradition are Norse in origin. Indeed, *St Magnus Cathedral* in Kirkwall is really a great Scandinavian church, founded in 1137 and already established as a glorious building when the isles became Scottish in 1468. It is both the symbol and the inheritance of the Viking occupation which the Orcadian poet, Edwin Muir, in his book *A Scottish Journey,* called 'the golden period of Orkney history, when Kirkwall was the capital of the Norse Western Empire'. Today it is the pride of Orkney, whose people and council have worked hard and successfully to keep it in good repair, and it is also the home of a congregation of the Kirk. It ranks with *Glasgow Cathedral* and *St Giles',* but there is a brightness and lightness about its red and white freestone that make it some visitors' preference. Karl Baedeker, series editor of the

King's College Chapel, Aberdeen

well-known guide-books, called Kirkwall 'a clean but dull town'. *St Magnus Cathedral* certainly improves on that reputation.

Another building admired just as much is *King's College Chapel* in Aberdeen, where the university services are held. Its tower, with the crown steeple (1500) is a joy, a 'crown on flying arches'. For those who like such pleasures, there is also some very elaborate woodwork and a flamboyant west window. Also in Old Aberdeen (well away from the city centre) is *St Machar's Cathedral* (1378-1552), said to be the only granite cathedral in the world, with twin towers completed by octagonal sandstone steeples. The big church in Union Street which looks like the city's cathedral is *St Nicholas,* the biggest pre-Reformation parish church in Scotland.

Aberdeen's granite gives distinction even to some quite plain churches; there are some elaborations in the suburbs and at Marischal College, where *G r e y f r i a r s   C h u r c h* is architecturally part of that granite array of pinnacles which is

St John's Kirk, Perth

English perpendicular in style, but late Victorian in creation. Also plain, but justifiably famous, is *Crathie Kirk* on Deeside, near Balmoral Castle. The best-known family in the congregation is the Royal Family who are regular attenders while residing at Balmoral.

Like Aberdeen, Dundee has a big city-centre church which looks like a cathedral. In fact it is two churches, *St Mary's* and *The Steeple*. (Until a few years ago there was a third one in the middle.) On the outskirts of Dundee there is also the very distinctive *Barnhill St Margaret's* church, now housing a lively mainstream suburban congregation but, in its early days, the cause of many arguments and Church lawsuits concerning 'Scoto-catholicism' in the Kirk. The building was designed to give scope for liturgical experiment and was decorated with symbolism which even liturgical enthusiasts find difficult to unravel!

Also in Tayside, Perth has surprisingly few really old buildings for so ancient and fair a city. But *St John's Kirk,* much restored, dates from 1450 and was the scene of John Knox's dramatic sermon against idolatry in 1559, which was the occasion (or excuse?) for the violent, angry, destructive streak in the Scots Reformation.

Stirling has a rather unusual historic church beside the castle: the *Church of the Holy Rude* (or Cross). Both Mary, Queen of Scots, and her son, James VI and I, were crowned in infancy there, the latter coronation being enhanced by a sermon from 'Master Knox'. (It clearly did more good for Scotland than for the infant king.) But the greatest church building in the Stirling area is a few miles to the north, *Dunblane Cathedral;* today one of the strongest parish churches of the Kirk. Beside it is the ecumenical Scottish Churches House, formed from the old houses of the square or close. Most of the *Dunblane Cathedral* building dates from the 13th century, but the tower has earlier Norman claims. John Ruskin, the Victorian art and social critic, was much impressed by the West Front with its tall lancet windows. The Cathedral is found at one gateway to the Highlands. At another gateway, on the Tay, stands *Dunkeld Cathedral,* whose 14th century choir section of the

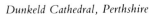
Dunkeld Cathedral, Perthshire

structure serves as a parish church. The congregation of the small town works hard to maintain their living part of the ancient building. The ruined part is carefully cared for at public expense!

Around the cathedral the battle of 1689 was fought in which the Covenanters' successors (by that time soldiers of King William III) checked the Highland advance which had been victorious further up-river at Killicrankie. *Dunkeld Cathedral*, with its lovely Tayside setting, is one of the many surprises waiting for anyone who looks seriously at Scotland's interesting churches. And there are many others. There is the ornate, early 19th century *St Mungo's, Alloa,* for example. At Culloden, near the battlefield, there is the *Barn Church,* which is quite literally an old barn turned into a church and skilfully adapted for a new congregation in a developing community. There is the tiny *Dornoch Cathedral* in Sutherland, and the cluster of fine churches in East Lothian which are miniature cathedrals in style if not in name. These churches which are from the

Dornoch Cathedral, Sutherland

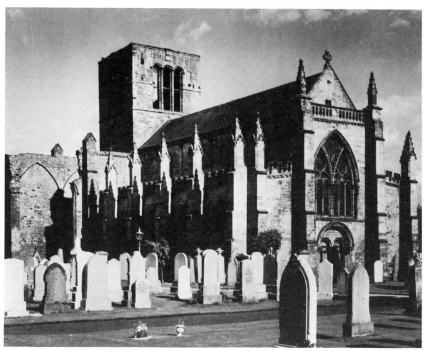

St Mary's, Haddington, East Lothian

pre-Reformation period include *Whitekirk and Tyninghame St Mary's, Pencaitland*, and *St Mary's, Haddington* ('the lamp of Lothian', which has had a notable modern restoration). There is also a good example of a post-Reformation church at Gifford, *Yester Kirk*.

In another part of Scotland, there is the 19th century *St Giles'* in Elgin, with its surprising Grecian portico. The ancient cathedral itself suffered many afflictions before the Reformation and was allowed to decay after it.

Neglect, on the heels of destruction during the English wars, also turned the Border abbeys into romantic ruins, but Kelso and Jedburgh have churches of interest, and Melrose has a fine kirk in a setting which must gladden the heart of any rugby man. Beside the Greenyards, the lovely ground made famous by the 'sevens' invented by local butcher Ned Haig, is *St Cuthbert's,* an elegant church of this century. The whole view enriches one of Scotland's finest small towns, with the Tweed only a stone's throw away and the kirk set on the slope above the rugby ground. And just across the Eildon Hills, above Melrose, is a jewel of a country church, *Bowden Kirk:* a good example of how a building of modest pretentions and much historic interest can be enhanced by its surroundings.

Yet if anyone is to get a truly comprehensive idea of the Scots Church, he must see merit in kirks with less prepossessing surroundings. They may be jammed into gaps in rows of Glasgow tenements, or set in bleak Highland landscapes (like *Kilbrandon and Kilchattan* on Seil Island, with its superb modern stained glass), or found in drab housing estates.

Reid Memorial Church, Blackford, Edinburgh

In post-WW2 settings, the churches tend to look less solid than in pre-WW2 ones. Money for church extension was not so tight before 1939, and some visually striking buildings were constructed: for example, at Knightswood in Glasgow. Of the same inter-war period (although not 'church extension' in the strictest sense) is the *Reid Memorial Church* at Blackford, in Edinburgh. It is unusual because it has a cloister and because it demonstrates the kind of skills and resources that the later Victorians had.

The duller Victorian kirks still in use, and the plain buildings of the 1930s and the post-war era (some good, most fair, a few awful), often have more vigorous congregations than some of the historic churches. These Victorian kirks are best acknowledged for their place in the life of the community, not only during Sunday worship, but on week-nights as well, when the various 'organisations' keep them lit up (and add to the soaring fuel bills!). *Claremont* and other churches in East Kilbride, *St Mungo's* in Cumbernauld, or *St*

Holy Trinity, Wester Hailes, Edinburgh

Mark's on the outskirts of the Lanarkshire steel town of Wishaw, are all good examples. East Kilbride, with Glenrothes and Cumbernauld, incorporate churches which make a good show of the parish system in new towns. Livingston, however, has a different pattern, with an 'ecumenical parish' and shared churches. Different styles of sharing are also to be found in two of the developing suburbs of Aberdeen: Episcopal and Roman Catholic congregations share the new Westhills church with the Kirk, and at the Bridge of Don, a new church (starting as part of *St Machar's Cathedral* but due to become a parish of its own) has been built, sharing amenities with a Roman Catholic church next door.

If you want to see the Church in areas where members are fewer in proportion to population, but where parish needs are at least as great, there are the Easterhouse churches in Glasgow, or *Holy Trinity,* Wester Hailes, in Edinburgh. These are not architectural jewels in the Kirk's crown, but they have a character that comes from their ministry,

their people, and the communities they serve. Like the duller side of Victoriana in many Glasgow and Edinburgh parishes, the face of the buildings sometimes conceals the virtues of the people who make up the congregation. These churches are seen to best advantage by a sympathetic visitor ready to join the congregation, especially to worship 'in spirit and in truth'.

Despite the considerable heritage of buildings, Scotland possibly lacks the full richness and variety of cathedrals and churches found in some European countries, including

England. But we rightly cherish what we have. Yet occasionally we underestimate parts of our inheritance or appreciate other parts only when (as with the best Victorian buildings) it is almost too late.

There are some notable Scots churches outside Scotland. Most Presbyterian churches founded by Scots now belong, of course, to local Churches, but in Madras or Melbourne or Montreal, the mark of the Scots connection remains, often in the style of building as well as the style of worship. Of the kirks outside Scotland that are still, in the strictest sense, in the Church of Scotland, there is the modern *St Columba's Pont Street* in London, with its curious cupola structure (well seen from the back of Harrods) surmounted by a cross set above the saltire. The other Scots kirk in London, *Crown Court, Covent Garden,* traces its descent from an ancient London church, or chapel, of the Crown of Scotland, but the building (more impressive inside than outside) is early 20th century.

Several of the Kirk's European churches have a distinguished setting: for example, the venerable 'English Reformed' Church in Amsterdam, or the Geneva *Auditoire* where Calvin lectured beside his cathedral of *St Peter*. In Paris, the Kirk in the Rue Bayard (near the Champs Elysées) was rebuilt after WW2, when its minister was still Donald Caskie, the war-time 'Tartan Pimpernel'. There are also Scots Churches (linked to the local Reformed tradition) in both Jersey and Guernsey. Much further away, Bermuda's historic Presbyterian Christ Church (which has an English Puritan tradition) is also an island outpost of the Church of Scotland. But without doubt, the most moving of the Scots churches abroad is *St Andrew's,* Jerusalem; so moving indeed (especially when dawn appears over the Old City across the Valley of Hinnom) that we may have to remind ourselves that there is no special sanctity in places and that Christ's presence is no more real in Jerusalem than anywhere else. He makes all places holy, as well as all things new.

But there is a proper place in the Christian life for buildings and in the Christian heart for 'taking pleasure in the stones' of Zion.

Today these can be expensive pleasures. Some countries solve their own Church's problems by lavish State contributions to historic churches or by letting even the most nominal Christians help pay the cost through a voluntary church tax. Scotland depends mainly on contributions from regular church attenders. This means that the Church will continue to reduce the number of buildings used for worship, and perhaps wrong local choices will sometimes be made. A less historic or duller building may be kept because it is cheaper to maintain and to heat than a more important one. But fortunately the last 20 years have seen a revival of interest in Scotland's heritage of church buildings, and a desire, not just among regular church-goers, to maintain it.

St Andrew's, Jerusalem

The way the Kirk works

3

The General Assembly and its Moderator

The General Assembly of the Church of Scotland, which meets for a week in Edinburgh every May, is the Kirk's Parliament, supreme court, and top tier of government. Its chairman, like those of the lesser courts of the Kirk, is called a Moderator. It is often, and wrongly, considered to be a gathering of ministers. Half the 1200 or so representatives of the Presbyteries are elders. All of them (elders and ministers) are known as 'commissioners'.

Assembly Week in Edinburgh still proves to be a social occasion, partly because of the entertaining and visiting done by the Queen's representative, the Lord High Commissioner. He resides for the week at the Palace of Holyroodhouse (at the opposite end of the Royal Mile from Edinburgh Castle) and attends the Assembly for much of its time. His arrival for the formal opening is a stately and ceremonial occasion, with heralds and a guard of honour. Those who like tradition or pageantry, or both, enjoy the ceremony. He also customarily invites Assembly commissioners (and other guests) to a garden party in the grounds of Holyroodhouse.

The Assembly, however, does not really need the Queen's Commissioner. He, or she, is its most distinguished visitor but is, strictly speaking, no more than that. The custom (not the rule) is that he, or she, addresses the Assembly at the start of its proceedings and then again just before the end. This is 'at the will of the Assembly'. He usually has something useful and acceptable to say, and the nomination of the Lord High Commissioner (on Government advice) is carefully made. Very often the Queen's representative is someone well-known to the Assembly; perhaps a past member of it, or himself deeply involved in the Church's local affairs in some way.

On very special occasions the Queen may attend in person, as she last did in her Silver Jubilee year, 1977. This adds to the colour, pageantry, the interest, and the pleasure. But it does not change the rules. The Church has a great respect for the Crown and the monarch, and a theological concern with proper government in the realm of what its confession calls 'the civil magistrate'. But it does not allow Government supremacy or interference in spiritual matters.

The Assembly could meet where and when it chose. At one critical moment in Scottish history (1638) it met in Glasgow and proceeded to upset King Charles I's plans for the Scottish Church. It still sees two realms in Scotland: that of the Crown and that 'of King Jesus'.

The Assembly opens after the pageantry, but soon settles down to work. It receives reports from its boards and committees; accepting, rejecting, adding to, or amending resolutions (called 'deliverances') proposed by them. It passes Church laws; legislative Acts which stipulate how the Church is to operate. It can also make decisions concerning petitions (sent in by anyone), and deal with any 'overtures' from the regional

Church councils, the Presbyteries.

The General Assembly settles cases, acting as supreme Church Court of Appeal. These may refer to humdrum matters: a congregation that does not want to unite with another, for example, or one which has had some quarrel with the Presbytery. But they may also refer to matters of dramatic importance: for example, an elder who is in trouble because he does not agree with the Church's practice on infant Baptism; or a minister who is appealing against a Presbytery decision to sack him from his parish; or, as happened in 1984, a murderer who, having served his sentence, wanted to become a minister and successfully asked that he should not be barred. Most Assembly debates concern what everyone regards as Church matters, but a large part of one day is set aside for a Church and Nation report, which is largely concerned with what some people would regard as politics: unemployment, nuclear weapons, the government of Scotland. Sometimes local issues and concerns get tagged on to the larger issues, so that a day when powerful passions have been stirred on pacifism or disarmament may end with an earnest resolution in defence of the BBC Scottish Symphony Orchestra.

The Assembly is sometimes called the nearest thing to a Parliament Scotland has had since the Union of 1707. Not all of its members approve of this view (although it is usually intended as flattery) for they fear that it distracts public interest away from the Assembly's more vital rôle in governing the Church.

As a debating, legislating and judicial chamber, however, the Assembly does merit some outside interest, not only for its place in Scottish life, but also for some of its distinctive characteristics. It is hard to think of any similar body which allows such scope to the individual member, even the Assembly clown and the Assembly bore. Although the length of speeches is limited (except in legal cases and doctrinal matters) it affords vast scope for impromptu amendments. There are also two apparently contradictory characteristics which go surprisingly well together: the Assembly will hear, and insist on a hearing for, very personal, unpopular or idiosyncratic views, but when it thinks a debate on a major issue has gone on long enough and that fresh speeches would simply be a repetition of old arguments, it can produce a cry of 'Vote, Vote', which is more fearsome than anything done under a parliamentary guillotine. When a speaker wanders over his time this can also, even before the Moderator imposes silence, produce a devastating rumble of feet which no-one mistakes for applause more than once!

It is also a far less predictable body than most parliamentary, or even Church, assemblies. One reason for this is its sheer size. In legal cases, for example, it becomes the world's largest jury. Another reason is the constant change in its composition. Ministers attend roughly one year in three, although a small group of officials are there *ex-officio* (former Moderators are virtually *ex-officio* members, although appointed by Presbyteries), and some other enthusiasts seem to manage to get themselves sent by their Presbyteries every year. Elders range between the hardy, annual attenders and a very large number who attend perhaps only one General Assembly in their lives. That inevitably makes it difficult for them to contribute fully, although these occasional attenders can sometimes produce remarkable speeches on areas of deep, personal knowledge or experience.

The General Assembly is influenced but not controlled by its leaders. But ordinary members matter very much. They are the people who have to be impressed by what the speakers choose to say or not say, as the case may be. And in the General Assembly, despite a tendency for official reports to have the edge on critics from the floor, debating has still to be a matter of persuasion.

There is often lobbying, but there is very little to resemble the rôle of parliamentary whips. When a vote is needed, members stand up to show if they are for or against. Only if this does not clearly indicate who has a majority, is there a count. This is done after tellers have collected voting slips.

The Moderator

The principal representative and spokesman (or perhaps in the future, spokeswoman) for our Church is the Moderator of the General Assembly. He is, as the title suggests, a chairman and not a chief executive. After the end

The Right Reverend Dr David Smith

of the General Assembly (where he is chairman, with former Moderators as deputies) it is now customary for him to visit some Presbyteries of the Church and to represent the Kirk during various events at home and overseas. He also provides statements when custom or special occasion or pressure of some sort may require that a personal voice should be heard speaking on behalf of the Kirk. A custom is also emerging by which he signs statements issued on behalf of Scottish or British 'Church leaders'.

The Moderator is respected as well as honoured in the Kirk, both for his office as well as for himself. But outsiders tend to exaggerate his importance. So too do members of the Kirk who write asking him to deal with anything they dislike, from the rejection of a candidate to the ministry, to the union of two congregations. Such letters either receive a non-commital reply or are passed on to the relevant boards and committees, which means that in practice it is probably an executive secretary who handles them.

The actual election at the

Assembly is a formality. The real voting is held in private before the nominee is put forward unanimously by a selection committee, although discreet lobbying for and against candidates is far from unknown.

By custom (and only custom) a Moderator is called Right Reverend and after he has served his term, Very Reverend.

Modern media techniques cause problems for a Church which is run by committees and councils. The media are always looking for a leader, and if not a leader, at least a spokesman. Authoritarian Churches, old-fashioned though they are in other ways, are admirably suited to provide these leaders. Even the choice of Pope in the Roman Catholic Church probably now involves conscious decisions about the 'image' that the Church wants to project. The Church of Scotland could conceivably have responded to these pressures by building up the rôle of a permanent chief executive. Some other Presbyterian Churches abroad have such an executive, but the Kirk has preferred to see the Moderator of the General Assembly, who changes annually, become a kind of archbishop on a one-year contract. But he must never be called Head of the Church: that title in the Reformed Churches belongs to Jesus Christ alone. Nor is he usually the most powerful or influential man in the Kirk. He does not chair committees while in office, although his previous rôle in committee work may have secured his election. In practice nowadays, most Moderators are not even left with much time to do their usual job, which is generally as a parish minister; although ministers in other fields, especially professors, can also be chosen for the post. Theoretically the Moderator does not need to be a minister. The Kirk's laws, although not its custom, would allow it to follow the example of various other Presbyterian Churches, where the Moderator has been an elder. So far, however, there has been only one exception to the custom, which is nearly a rule. Shortly after the Reformation, the great Scots scholar, George Buchanan, one of the most famous Europeans of his time, served a term as Moderator, but he was a 'doctor' or professor which is not really equivalent to a modern layman.

Most of the great leaders of the Kirk have been Moderators, beginning with John Knox. Nineteenth-century Moderators included Thomas Chalmers, who was called to the chair again in the Free Church which emerged from the Disruption. Twentieth-century Moderators, whose election really recognised their fame rather than created it, have included such diverse Christians as George MacLeod (Lord MacLeod of Fuinary) and Professor Tom Torrance, the internationally-famous theologian.

In modern times, it has not been usual practice to give a Moderator a second term. An exception perhaps, was John White, the greatest single architect of the reunion of the Kirk in 1929. He was Moderator in the old 'established' Kirk and was similarly honoured again by the reunited one. A few outstanding men, however, have somehow been passed over or have declined nomination. The

The Very Reverend John Paterson

most recent significant refusal was by the great biblical communicator, Professor William Barclay. Occasionally an eminently suitable man will decline nomination because his wife's health or temperament might not stand the strain which the year of hectic engagements can impose. The Moderator's wife is expected to play a supporting rôle. Bachelors may still get elected, but not very often.

Just possibly, although there is no hard evidence, other potential Moderators may have declined nomination because they do not like the curious costume: tricorn hat, lace-ruff, swallow-tail coat, breeches, silk or similar stockings, and buckled shoes. From time to time, people in the Kirk denounce the costume as embarrassing and absurd, but Moderators themselves seem to come to terms with it. It is distinctive, easily recognisable, and no more bizarre than the various adaptations of the nightshirt favoured by some other denominations.

Presbyteries

The name 'presbytery' is derived from the Greek *presbyteros,* meaning older person or elder. Most Presbyterians see 'presbyters' as being either ministers or 'lay' elders. In some other Churches, 'presbyter' is almost a synonym for clergyman; a view also taken by some of our ministers with 'high' or ecumenical views. However, African Presbyterians like to call their elders 'presbyters', to avoid confusion between village and church elders.

It is not surprising that the Presbytery should be a basic unit in the kind of Church which, in English, is called Presbyterian. A Presbytery is an area executive council of the Church, made up of ministers and representative elders from the congregations in the area. There are also elders (called 'freely elected') chosen by the Presbytery to make sure that retired and specialist ministers entitled to membership do not outnumber the elders.

The Presbyteries vary enormously in size, from a handful of congregations to a very large number: for example, the Glasgow and Edinburgh ones. (Glasgow has been called 'the largest Presbytery in the world'.) Some meet monthly, some much less frequently. Some of their business is involved with the routine administration of the Church. They approve the movement of ministers in and out of congregations; license new ministers and, after a probationary period, ordain them, usually when they are called (and elected) to parishes for the first time. They also supervise candidates for the ministry, although it is arguable how effective or important this function now is. Their work also concerns the local devolution of national schemes. For example, they allocate what each congregation ought to contribute to the budget of the Church.

Presbyteries also have a veto on changes in the constitutional law of the Church. These have to be considered by the General Assembly but, under the Barrier Act, if a majority are against the proposal, it automatically fails. For some basic matters of the Kirk's constitution and doctrine, a far more exacting procedure is involved, with Presbyteries considering matters twice. Here, the support of two-thirds of the Presbyteries, as well as the General Assembly, is required before a change can be effected.

Between Presbyteries and the General Assembly there is another tier of Church courts called the Synods. They are far less important, although it is possible for appeals against certain kinds of Presbytery decisions to go to the Synod. Presbyteries remain the vital connection between the national superstructures of the Church (General Assembly, boards and executive staff) and the local foundations of the Church. They usually function quite adequately as part of the Kirk's administration, law-making, and in the settlement of disputes.

Whether they function quite so well in the provision of leadership and inspiration is less clear. The fairest verdict here may be this: some do, some do not.

The Parish and its congregation

The term 'parish' is derived from a Greek word meaning district. Once it was the unit for local government and social service functions as well as for church affairs. But Scotland no longer has any need for 'civil parishes' and the Kirk's parish system differs in important respects from the one it inherited at the Reformation and developed afterwards. Today a parish is the territory within which a congregation of the Church has a special responsibility, with special obligations on the minister and kirk session.

The modern Kirk is a union of those who kept the old parish system and of the Presbyterians who had opted out of it, gathering themselves into new congregations. Sometimes you can still hear a particular Church in an area (usually the oldest) being referred to as 'the parish church'. In many Scots towns, there is a central kirk whose title is 'The Old Parish Church' or something similar to that. It may once have been the only church of the town. There is also much debate among members of the Kirk concerning the rôle of

'gathered congregations', as distinct from 'territorial' ones. Is it a good idea to encourage 'gathered congregations' (perhaps very evangelical) which attract people who like that particular style, rather than attracting those who just happen to live in the vicinity of the church in question?

But although every 'charge' of the Church of Scotland is a parish church (apart from such special cases as congregations of deaf people), no rules prevent members from gathering in any church that takes their fancy. If they do not like the minister, they can 'lift their lines'. This is the vernacular phrase for resigning from a congregation, usually with the intention of moving to another.

In the countryside and small towns, it is now fairly clear where a church's parish lies. The problem is often that one minister has to handle two or three, even four, parishes; some of those being composed of two former smaller parishes. No wonder, for example, people sometimes talk of Upper Tweeddale parishes when they mean the linked charge (as the Kirk calls it) of 'Broughton, Glenholm and Kilbucho linked with Skirling linked with Stobo and Drumelzier linked with Tweedsmuir'. It is both a mouthful and a handful!

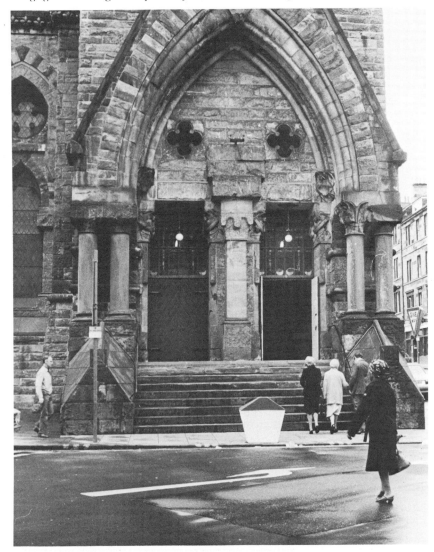

Congregation entering Barclay-Bruntsfield Church, Edinburgh

But even in the cities and large towns, there are often very artificial parish boundaries, the result of the multiplication of Presbyterian Churches in the past and the steady reduction in their numbers since 1929. The map of parish boundaries in Glasgow or Edinburgh is still constantly changing. Even in some thriving and expanding suburban areas where several churches are needed, they may, for historical reasons, be built quite close together. They are allotted segments of new housing areas which have sprung up around them, but which are often some distance away from the church itself.

The theory of the parish system maintains that a local church has a territorial area in which it has a missionary job to do, and in which it has a duty to help everyone who lives there, including those who are not affiliated to the Kirk. This concept works best when the area of the parish has a real sense of community. Ministers are expected to be scrupulous about 'intruding' into another minister's parish, although this does not apply to pastoral care for members of their own congregation living outside the parish, as quite often happens in the cities. They also try to respond to anyone seeking their help and services in the parish: perhaps, for example, when a parishioner who may never have come to church, dies, and the family would like a Christian funeral.

But the main problems of the parish today are not legal but evangelical. The church is both a visible building and a congregation of people, some of whom never seem to be away from the kirk and some who come rarely or not at all. The church is also inevitably associated, for better or worse, with the style, personality, strength and weaknesses of its parish minister, as well as the attitudes of the elders and the rest of the hard-core congregation. Some churches get a local reputation for being warm, friendly and welcoming; others for being cold or stand-offish. It is not easy today for the minister to reach people who are rarely or never in church to hear a sermon;

good, bad or middling. But there are sermons in what you do as well as what you say, even in the way you look or smile. This applies to elders as much as ministers, pehaps even more.

Almost every congregation has a Sunday school. Most have other youth organisations or clubs. Often the majority of the boys and girls come from families which are not on the communicant roll. At the other end of the age range, congregations usually support old people of the parish as well as their own elderly members. There may be a system of visiting, or of 'street wardens'. Or the church hall itself may be the best place (sometimes the only place) for community organisations and clubs to meet. In the cold, economic climate of the 1980s many congregations have also had to consider what they could do for people out of work, although there are mixed feelings about clubs for the unemployed. Not everyone who is without a job wishes to meet only people with the same problem. Local churches have often been able to help in

practical, job-creation projects, even (as in one remarkable case in Gilmerton, Edinburgh) to sponsor a substantial job-training scheme, or (as in Dundee) to provide a centre to help the handicapped. There are also a number of parishes where the church has a more specific and local, as well as national, rôle in social work. The minister, deaconess, or other 'parish assistant' or lay missionary, can be a source of help and advice. There are often benevolent funds which are important for modest practical help and, perhaps at Christmas, as a gesture of care and concern.

All this is part of the mission of the local church which gathers on Sunday for its weekly festival. How effective that mission is depends not only on the personal qualities and preaching ability of the minister, but also on the team-work of the congregation, both in numbers and energy. Sometimes the differences between strong and weak local churches seem inexplicable in terms of economics, or even when the talents of the minister as an individual are taken into consideration. But the effectiveness of the kirk session as the leaders of the congregation (and, in some things, the supporter of the minister) may be what counts.

The kirk session is composed of the minister and the elders; perhaps only three or four in a tiny country congregation, or up to 100 in a very big city or suburban one. (Elders are ordained lay members of the church — see later chapter.) Sometimes the session (the parish church council) handles all the affairs of the congregation, including all the financial problems of the building, and of fund-raising. More often now there are members of the congregation elected to form a financial management board with the elders. A few churches retain the more congregational style of government in the United Presbyterian tradition, in which the minister (permanent moderator of the kirk session) does not intrude on 'temporal' affairs and there is a sharp distinction between elders handling 'spiritual' matters and managers dealing with 'temporal'

ones. The lay chairman of this kind of board may be called a 'preses'. Elsewhere the board may be called a 'deacons' court' and ordained deacons are roughly equivalent to managers.

Most parishes do not tackle their work in complete isolation, quite apart from the guidance and overall control of the Presbytery. Much depends on the geographical situation and the local ecumenical climate. At one extreme is the 'ecumenical parish' in Livingston, West Lothian; a new town where an experiment in co-operation among Churches has involved sharing buildings with other Protestant denominations. At the other extreme are congregations which have little to do with their neighbours or perhaps have no near neighbours at all, which is often the case in country districts. There are parishes, suburban as well as rural, where the only church building of any kind is the parish kirk. But in between are many degrees of co-operation between neighbouring Church of Scotland parishes and other denominations (no longer just Protestant ones) either through

local councils of churches or on a church-to-church basis.

The parish and the congregation within it is the basic unit of the Church as its people see it. Most of them have knowledge of the Church only through its local life and their own personal experience of it. Even among the elders, only a minority ever take part in Presbytery or General Assembly decision-making. Church politicians and lawyers tend to see things differently, emphasising how fundamental the Presbytery is to a Presbyterian Church. They also highlight the rights of appeal and powers of decision that give the General Assembly its rôle as a supreme court. Presbyterianism can be fairly centralised in some matters, but the congregation, working and worshipping in the parish, is what most people encounter first and foremost. It is also the place where the ambiguous word 'democracy' has a clearer application in the Kirk.

How 'democratic' the Kirk is, depending on definitions, can be a matter for argument. There are elements of democracy at all levels, but in the congregation they are easier to find. Elders can be elected by the congregation (although in some congregations, it is the session which elects new members to its ranks). In the kirk session, the elders heavily outnumber their ministerial moderator. More important is the right of the people to elect their own minister; a right which was fought hard for and painfully won at earlier stages of the Kirk's history. It is still a right which is exercised, and sometimes the congregation overturns the nomination of its vacancy selection committee, or votes against him with a majority which makes the nominee back down even before the final decision to uphold the election ('sustain the call') is due to be taken by the Presbytery.

Once elected, it is a different story for the minister. He is normally secure in his parish unless the Presbytery decides otherwise, and it can only act to remove him on clear grounds of default; moral, doctrinal or practical. The Presbytery can act under very complicated church law if the minister has got his parish into a hopeless mess or, under recent and still untested provisions, if redevelopment, or some similar change in the social landscape, has utterly changed the situation to which he was called.

Some people may think ministers too secure! However, ministers believe they have to be protected from quarrels and factions, to which all human beings are prone, and from the temptation to seek the wrong kind of popularity. Certainly the security and stability of the parish minister, with tenure comparable to that of the English vicar or rector, is one of the elements which shapes the style and character of the Scots ministry and the life of the Scots congregation.

A Kirk Session Meeting

Ministers

There are about 1350 parish ministers in Scotland, a few hundred more who are retired but still members of the Presbytery, and perhaps a couple of hundred others working in specialised jobs, but still very conscious of their ordination. The latter may be university or school teachers, Chaplains to the Forces, specialist chaplains, Church officials, even broadcasters. Many of them take an active part in Presbytery and General Assembly work. It is the parish minister, however, who typifies most people's notion of a 'real minister'. His job is the one which people still identify as the minister's work: preaching on Sundays, visiting the congregation and parish (especially the sick at home or in hospital) and conducting funerals, weddings, and baptisms. But a minister may also be a school chaplain or a part-time hospital or industrial chaplain as well. In our Church he is called the 'minister of Word and Sacraments.' He takes the main responsibility for preaching, and only ordained ministers are allowed to conduct the services for the two Sacraments.

In the Kirk all ministers are equal. There is parity among ministers, with no special ranks or orders. Whether in practice some ministers become much more equal than others is often a cause for Presbyterian argument! But there is probably a general desire to maintain that principle of 'parity', even although some ministers wish they had a 'pastor of pastors' to turn to sometimes. However, Presbytery clerks and experienced church officials may meet this need.

Ministers are ordained for life, although the actual ordination (as distinct from licensing to preach) does not usually occur until a man or woman is appointed to a parish or a specialised post requiring ordination. The Kirk does not have curates, although young ministers serve a year or two as assistants. There is also a modern trend in bigger parishes towards 'associate ministers': for example, ordained mature men and women, who are sometimes even semi-retired (although in this case, they may revert to the title of assistant minister).

Another modern trend seeks 'new forms of ministry'. Those which are already firmly established include full-time chaplains to hospitals, universities and even industries. A more recent development involves 'community ministers', seen as a new form of 'parish' ministry. Their rôle varies according to the kind of community they serve, but it can include work with schools, youth groups or old people.

An even more recent development is the 'auxiliary' minister; ordained, but unpaid and working in another trade or profession to earn a living. This is a different concept from that of the full-time 'lay missionary' who could, in practice, be an assistant minister; or the 'reader', who is what other churches might call a lay preacher. There are different ideas in the Church about the potential of this new concept which has not yet had time to make its impact in more than a few parts of Scotland.

Industrial chaplain

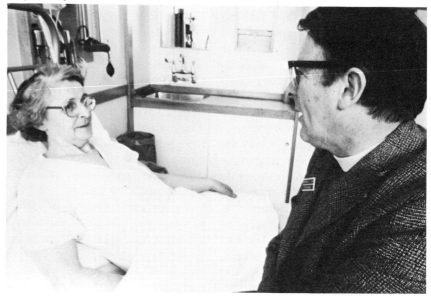

Army chaplain

Community minister

Hospital chaplain

Elders

Elders are the local councillors of the Kirk, but they are also much more. When they are first appointed, they are 'ordained'; the same term is used for ministers. An elder's appointment follows an election, either by the congregation or by the kirk session. This elders' ordination does not fulfil the same function as a minister's, but it is meant as a special commitment, and a life-long one.

Elders are not reordained if they move house and are admitted to the kirk session in a new parish, nor if they resume duty later after resigning from active membership of their kirk session. So far, the Kirk (unlike some other Presbyterian Churches) has not taken to the idea of selecting elders only for a fixed term of years.

Variations occur in the way the kirk session and congregations are run. As already mentioned, in some older parish churches the elders alone, with the minister as their kirk session chairman or moderator, handle all the congregation's financial affairs. But more often now, they share in a wider board of management.

But the eldership is a 'spiritual office'. It is a commitment to share the 'rule' or government of the Church, and that includes rule in spiritual matters as well as temporal. During previous centuries in Scotland, members of the kirk session, and therefore the elders, spent much of their time administering discipline. This might not be to modern taste, especially when the kirk session was on the look-out for 'Sabbath-breakers'. But they also undertook many of the local welfare functions now dealt with by the State or local councils. They also had for a long time the job of supervising local education. Indeed, the great reformer, John Knox, wanted a school in every parish.

Elders also have an important pastoral rôle. Most of them have a responsibility for visiting districts, calling on church members (and often many others too), sometimes even acting as the channel of information and communication for the specialist pastor, the minister. There still remains a custom of visiting districts and leaving 'Communion cards', traditionally admission tokens, but nowadays really just invitation cards or reminders.

At Communion services, elders have a very visible rôle to play, although it is a matter of custom and not doctrine. They lift the bread and wine from the Table, and take it around the congregation to serve the people. Elders make up half the members of the Presbyteries (sometimes more than half when ministers are scarce) and half the General Assembly. At the Assembly, they sit with ministers on all doctrinal and disciplinary cases, as well as on matters of Church concern in social and public affairs.

It may also be worth saying what elders do not do! They do not (in the Church of Scotland) preside at a Communion service. That is the minister's function. Nor do they normally preach, although in many churches, elders may occasionally conduct an 'elders' service' at which one of

Elders at work

them may speak about his faith or work. However, a relatively small minority of elders are licensed to preach, not because they are elders, but because they are qualified as lay preachers (called 'readers' in the Kirk). But lay preaching in the Church of Scotland is used far less than in several other Protestant Churches, such as the Methodists.

Incidentally, despite their title, elders need not be venerable in looks or years. The minimum age is only 21! Most congregations try to ordain some elders in their twenties and thirties. Although it was not until the 1960s that women were declared eligible for the eldership, there has been since then a steady increase in the proportion of women elders. And the more general rôle of women in the Kirk forms the basis of the next chapter.

Women in the Kirk

The modern Kirk makes no distinction between women and men in its highest offices: the ministry and the eldership. No membership statistics are kept by sex, but it may be that the majority of Church members and regular attenders are women. Women constitute a slowly increasing minority of ministers, and a large and rapidly increasing minority of elders. Just over 40 per cent of elders now being ordained are women. The proportion of new ministers who are female is till under 20 per cent.

Traditionally the most influential office held by women in the Church (somewhere between a consultancy and an unpaid assistantship) was an unofficial one. It was created, or at least recognised, initially at the Reformation. It is the 'lady of the manse'. There is no bar on bachelors in our Church's ministry but the majority of men ministers are married. Many women ministers are also married, some with young children, but no pattern for a 'manse husband' has yet evolved to match the tradition of the manse wife.

The great majority of the women who belong to our Church have no such specialised rôle as minister, deaconess, elder, or even mother to the minister's bairns. The Church of Scotland does not have nuns, or monastic orders, either. Women may serve on boards and committees or, in thousands of cases, as Sunday school teachers. But in these rôles they take no commitment vows except as members, which of course means a very great commitment indeed.

Inevitably, the Church has reflected to a large extent the cultural patterns and expectations of society concerning the rôle of the sexes, although there were remarkable exceptions in the early centuries of the Reformed Church, just as there were in the mediæval Church. The most legendary of these, and one of the most interesting, was Jenny Geddes in the 17th century. She allegedly took direct action against the unpopular introduction of set prayer-book services in St Giles'; the High Kirk of Edinburgh. This was the result of an attempt by King Charles I to force his ideas on an unwilling Church. She may or may not have picked up her stool (in those days there were no pews) and hurled it at the King's tame preacher, but her protest certainly expressed the hostile reaction among the people at that time.

In the next century Willielma Maxwell, Lady Glenorchy, played a major part in evangelical revivals and helped sustain the missionary drive in the Highlands which made the area a stronghold of Calvinism.

There was a far more decisive female influence in the 19th century, notably through the creation in the 1880s of an order of deaconesses, and the establishment of the Woman's Guild, which remains a great force in both Scottish and Church life today.

Deaconesses still continue to serve in the modern Church, although the modern diaconate is now open to both sexes. It provides services in social work,

Reverend Margaret Forrester, St Michael's, Edinburgh

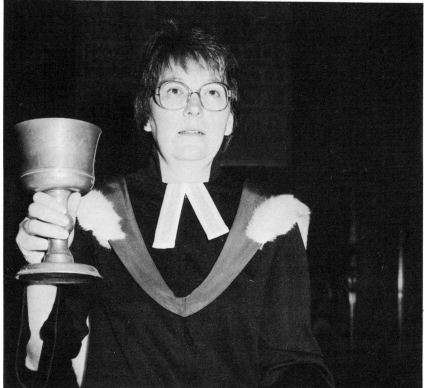

evangelism, Christian education and pastoral care, for example. The first of the Scots deaconesses was an aristocratic Victorian woman of saintly qualities, Lady Grisell Baillie.

The order of deaconesses (often serving in the same capacity as modern church social workers) were ahead of their time both in their methods of social work and in the theology which inspired their actions. Although Victorian theological assumptions ruled out the ordination of women, the creation of deaconesses was a conscious bid to give dedicated and specially commissioned women a share in the ministry of the whole Church and in its leadership. The astonishing thing is that it took nearly 80 years before the Kirk got round to accepting women as elders and, thanks to a challenge led by a deaconess called Mary Lusk (who was working as an assistant university chaplain), overcoming its hesitations about having them as ministers.

One reason for the long delay may have been the success of the other Victorian experiment, the Woman's Guild. There were relatively few deaconesses but the Guild provided hundreds of thousands of women with opportunities for service. It still exists today in almost all Church of Scotland congregations. Its nearest equivalent in England is the Mothers' Union, but the Scots Guild makes maternity optional. However, many churches have young women's groups (part of the Guild) mainly drawn from mothers of young children. The Guild's style, formal and informal, varies from place to place, and nationally from presidency to presidency. In the early 1980s for example, the Guild became involved in arguments about whether it was proper to pray to 'Our Mother God'. Most Guildswomen showed no such inclination but some, directly or through the office of the World Council of Churches, had been influenced by currents of feminism. They felt that some women were alienated from the Church by its male-dominated style, in language as well as government. Earlier, an inquiry by an *ad hoc*

From: *The Women's Missionary Magazine of the United Free Church of Scotland, 1908*

OUR OUTGOING MISSIONARIES

MISS ISABELLA CARMICHAEL
RAJPUTANA

MISS HELEN McMILLAN
M.B., Ch.B.,
RAJPUTANA

MISS ELSA DANIELSSON
NAGPUR

MISS MARY GRAY
RAJPUTANA

MISS CHRISTINA ROBERTSON
CALABAR

MISS ELLA PATERSON
RAJPUTANA

MISS AGNES COWAN
M.B., Ch.B.,
MANCHURIA

MISS ROSINA McMINN
CALABAR

General Assembly committee concerning the 'community of women and men', and the rôles of women and men in society, had veered in a similar direction. And with this in mind, Guild leaders (although not many ordinary members) even began at one stage to think aloud about whether an all-women organisation really had a future. But the notion of the Guild 'phasing itself out' was probably itself only a passing notion. The Guild remains a great positive force in the Church, in general and in its support for particular projects, with a highly developed 'delegate' system designed to keep local branches in touch with central Guild and Church activities.

The Guild's style is largely what the members locally choose to make it. They are often more resourceful than the Kirk at many things from prayers to fund-raising for especially worthy projects. They provide a focus for a vast voluntary effort and a great power for goodness. The constant problem now is how to meet the needs of older members and still encourage the younger women who go to church but who closely follow the trends of the present day.

Another area where women played a major dedicated rôle in the Church, long before it was possible for them to be ordained, was in overseas missionary work. The missionary's wife could never just be an ordinary wife and companion. Inevitably she was a missionary too, and sometimes she had even more hardship and heartache to bear than her husband. In the days before the development of modern tropical medicine, there were parts of the world which ought to have been called the White Woman's Grave, and it was often, very sadly, the grave of her children as well. There were many child deaths among missionary families.

Long before the end of the great missionary age, however, women were also working abroad as teachers, nurses and doctors. Perhaps the most remarkable Scots missionary was Mary Slessor of Dundee, who went to Calabar in 1876 and worked in Nigeria until her death in 1915, building up a remarkable, personal influence among the local people.

Many other Scots Presbyterian women were to have less spectacular, but just as effective rôles to fulfil, particularly as pioneers of women's education in India, China and various parts of Africa. They were often able to work in places where men were barred. And some who went out as professional missionary women soon found themselves in a position to adopt the new rôle of missionary wives as well.

This tradition of missionary work has helped to ensure that the modern Woman's Guild of the Kirk combines a worldwide outlook with local roots. Perhaps it has also helped to prepare the Church of Scotland for the step which most Anglican provinces, including the Church of England, and the entire Roman Catholic and Orthodox Churches, have yet to take: the ordination of women, and the removal of all barriers of sex discrimination within the ministry and other structures of the Church. This should not come as a surprise to anyone who takes into account the friendships Jesus Himself maintained with women, depicted in the Gospels. Nor

should it puzzle anyone who interprets St Paul's warnings (e.g. *I Corinthians*) to some young Churches, in the wider perspective given by the New Testament as a whole. Christians remember not only the special intimation of the happiest event to Mary, the Mother of our Lord, but remember also that it was women who received the first proclamation that Jesus was risen.

For it was 'the women who had followed Jesus from Galilee' (*Luke 23:55*) who returned to the tomb and found it empty. Then, remembering Jesus's words about death and resurrection, they returned from the sepulchre and told all these things to the disciples and to all the rest. They had believed before the men, and they had proclaimed their belief.

Christians should also be aware of the very evident community of women and men in the New Testament Church.

Women have an equally important rôle in the Church today. But time will show, now that all barriers in our Church have been removed, how far it will prove to be a different rôle from that of the men.

Sunday school and youth organisations

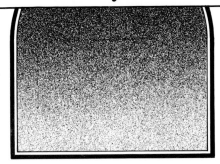

Half a century ago nearly half of Scotland's children went to a Presbyterian Sunday school. Today the figure is far lower; perhaps, in the roundest possible figure, only about 15 per cent. Even in primary classes it is not much above 20 per cent. There has been a reaction against the Victorian enthusiasm for the Sunday school. Although much more in the way of lively teaching and fresh thinking has gone into the organisation of modern Sunday schools, they have to work in a cool climate; sometimes even a hostile one.

But it is easy to underestimate the continuing scale and importance of the Kirk's youth work. At the end of 1984 there were more than 100 000 children aged 11 and under in Sunday schools, and just under 24 000 young people between 12 and 17 attending Bible classes. Another 12 000 went along to Boys' Brigade Bible classes. Nearly 20 000 young people belonged to Church-run youth clubs and 6500 to youth fellowships.

These figures overlap with others showing that about 112 000 young people in Scotland belong to uniformed youth organisations connected with the Church of Scotland's congregations. Of these, the senior one is the Boys' Brigade (BB); the pioneer uniformed youth organisation. It is internationally and inter-denominationally Christian, but its roots are to be found in Scottish Presbyterianism. Incidentally, its founder, Sir William Smith, was a member of a congregation whose minister was the father of John Reith, the first Director General of the BBC (1923-38). The BB began in a Glasgow church's mission hall. The Church link remains an essential part of the Boys' Brigade, as well as the Girls' Brigade. (However, the girls' movement has not yet matched the quite exceptional influence which Smith's movement has had on Scottish life, but its place in the Church and in Scottish life now seems secure.)

Many congregations have Scout and Girl Guide units, whereas Boys' and Girls' Brigade companies tend to be more evident in evangelical congregations, and (at least where the BB is concerned) in working-class ones. But it is not unusual to find that a congregation sponsors several youth organisations. Guides are often to be found in a congregation with a strong BB tradition, and it is not unknown for BB and church-sponsored Scouts to share the same meeting place.

There are no Scottish schools run by the Church of Scotland, except as part of its social work. This is because there is a long Scots tradition of public Christian-inspired education. John Knox wanted a school in every parish, and for three centuries kirk sessions sustained Scottish primary education. In the past century the main Scots educational stream consisted of 'public' schools (the term has a different meaning in Scotland and does not apply to independent or private schools) which were non-denominational, but

Christian nevertheless, although pupils belonging to other denominations, or to no religion at all, could be excused from Religious Instruction (now restyled Religious Education).

There has always been a good deal of diversity within the public i.e. the State provided sector, quite apart from the special provision made since 1918, by which Roman Catholic schools have achieved special status within the State system. (In practice, non-denominational schools are often just called Protestant schools.) Sometimes this diversity has been only too apparent in Religious Education, where the quality of teaching depends on the inclinations (or lack of inclination) of the teacher. Today however, Religious Education has become a subject which merits specialist teachers and even examinations, but its rôle is not yet entirely clear or universally agreed upon. Among the RE teachers there are a number of ministers of the Kirk, although ordinary parish ministers sometimes exercise great influence (if their aptitudes are right and the head teacher is

co-operative) as school chaplains. This is a rôle which can be what the minister decides to make it. He can choose actively to be involved or merely to carry out his duties in a minimal way. Staff school chaplains are only to be found in some independent schools, usually Scots schools similar to the kind of educational establishments which the English call 'public schools'.

Today the Kirk's main problem is probably its relationship with young people. It has not really closed the generation gap which opened up in the 1960s, although it has many vigorous youth groups and

Members of the Boy's Brigade

no scarcity of young applicants who wish to be considered as candidates for the ministry. It also shares in the active inter-denominational evangelical work of the Scripture Union in schools, and in the activities of the Christian Unions in universities and colleges. But, in the parishes and congregations, the picture is less optimistic, less well-defined, although it has its glimmers of light. In some parishes, it almost seems as though the Kirk has lost touch with young people. In others, there is a scarcity of young people because many have to leave home for work, even for secondary education. And yet, elsewhere the church halls may be full of young people every night of the week.

Even where youth organisations and activities remain vigorous, many of the Kirk's young people have not in recent years gone on to join as 'full' or communicant members by the vows or profession of faith which are regarded as confirming their admission to the Church at Baptism. One problem is that in the Church of Scotland, 'Confirmation' (a phrase used in

Children at Sunday School

parts of the Kirk) comes later than in continental Lutheran Churches for example. In those Churches a great many young people become full members and are not seen much around the Church again: their confirmation may take place too early to be meaningful to them. In the Kirk, a large number drift away several years before the age at which they would in earlier years have been expected to come to classes for 'new communicants'. One school of thought in the Kirk wants to encourage children to join in the Communion service with their families, but this has not won general support in the Church, so far.

Nevertheless, even in these years when young people have been reluctant to make formal commitments, there has remained a substantial flow of new Kirk members in their late teens and early twenties. Most of the 12 000 to 14 000 new communicants admitted in recent years probably still come from this age group, although the average age of joining may be higher than it used to be.

The Kirk's money

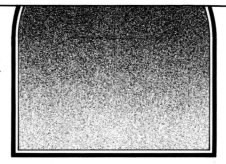

At one time, the main source of the Church of Scotland's income was the *teind* or *tithe,* which was based on a farming economy. Even in the early years of this century, the state of kirk funds in some parishes depended upon the price of corn. In those days, local proprietors in the parish (the 'heritors') had to maintain the church buildings.

But all that has long since changed. In the modern Church of Scotland, as in the 'free' or 'voluntary' Scots Presbyterian Churches of Victorian times, the main source of funds is the money which the people themselves give week by week. The income from the congregations (as reported in 1985) amounted to nearly £37 million out of the £46 million total annual income of the Kirk. This was derived mainly from collections, or covenants donated by individual members, and was supplemented by various fund-raising activities. Most money comes in by means of week-by-week envelopes which churchgoers hand over when a bag or plate is passed round. In most churches, this 'free will offering' is far greater than the loose pounds and pence in the collection.

It also seems now to be reviewed often enough to keep the Kirk a little ahead of inflation. The 1985 General Assembly was told there had been almost a 10 per cent increase on the previous years.

Most of this money is spent locally. The minister has to be paid (there is a complicated system by which poor and remote parishes are helped in this by all the rest) and the roof of the kirk has to be kept watertight. About £13 million of the £34 million congregational income in 1983 was spent on the various costs of maintaining the ministry throughout Scotland, including pensions and National Insurance. More than £17 million went on other expenditure, including the maintenance and heating of buildings. Only £3.2 million was left for what is called 'mission and service': education, social work, help for overseas churches (which used to be referred to as 'foreign missions'), Church extension, and home mission. Ecumenical organisations received only £100 000; three-quarters of it going to the British Council of Churches and the Scottish Council of Churches.

The 1984-85 improvement is unlikely to alter radically these proportions in the near future.

Finance is never quite as simple as it looks. The congregations of the Kirk are the largest groups of fund-raisers for Christian Aid in Scotland, and some of them support other world-aid bodies like Tear Fund. The very small social work section of the central Church budget (£300 000) is heavily supplemented when providing services which qualify for government or local authority subsidy, or when people make a contribution for services received: for example, in homes and hostels. Various Church efforts and agencies are also greatly helped by legacies, while a few (notably bookshops and publications) operate on ordinary commercial lines as trading accounts.

What is now very clear, however, is that the amount of Church work depends on what the people of the Church are ready to contribute. The 1985 reports shows that members contributed an average of 80p a week each, although that included everyone named on a roll. The figure for active members is appreciably higher, although not very high when compared to some smaller and very dedicated denominations. Even the improved 1985 figures suggest that 'active' members may average about £1 per week in direct offerings, with perhaps another 35p through special appeals and efforts.

But surely the Kirk owns a vast amount of property? Of course it does, but mainly in the form of churches and manses (ministers' houses) that have to be kept in repair. Try selling a redundant church and see what you get for it, especially if it is a listed building of historic or architectural interest!

In some countries with smaller proportions of people attending church, there is a voluntary church tax which enables the buildings to be maintained in some style, and Church work to be developed. There is nothing similar in Scotland, or in the rest of Britain for that matter. However, a few historic buildings (Glasgow Cathedral, for example) have special arrangements which enable them to be maintained in good order from public funds. Other buildings, more numerous, may be helped from time to time by historic buildings grants and various trusts. But the main burden, even in a small parish, falls on the people of the congregations. In Dunkeld, for example, the State keeps the ruined part of the ancient cathedral in good order, but the congregation in the small town (population 1000 or so) has to keep up the part that lives on as the parish church!

Social responsibility

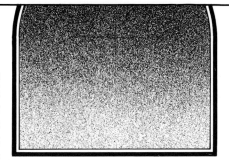

In the past, the Church was really Scotland's only social work agency. Before and after the Reformation, it had a responsibility to the poor, and it was the kirk sessions who used to provide what later generations would come to know as 'social security'. The Church pioneered many forms of social care where the State later followed and then often assumed responsibility. Today most of the Church of Scotland members in the caring professions are not employed by the Church, although their work may be one expression of their faith.

However, the Church's Social Responsibility Board still meets many needs, pioneers new ventures, and co-operates with government and local authority agencies. It employs more than 1200 people in this work. For example, it has 39 eventide homes for old people, and a home for 'elderly mentally confused'. (It offers Scotland's only residential care for sufferers of senile dementia.) It has five young people's hostels; four hostels for alcoholics; one each for epileptics, mentally handicapped adults, and mentally handicapped children. It runs three 'List D' schools for children with special problems; two night shelters for the homeless; two emergency hostels, and three counselling centres. The Board even planned the first residential units in Scotland to care for drug addicts.

The Church also took the lead in sponsoring the Kirk Care Housing Association and many congregations also co-operate, in one way or another, with sheltered housing projects for old people. And their pastoral care and community interests display a strong sense of social responsibility which strives to meet local and personal needs.

Ministers, lay missionaries and deaconesses also find that they often have to be counsellors; spiritual and practical needs can often be linked. That link is being discovered (or perhaps re-discovered) in health and healing, an area of new Christian growth and interest which is being reflected in the Kirk.

But the social responsibility of the Christian is not only, or even mainly, a matter of Church organisation. It is also a concern both of personal conscience and society's values. Sometimes this can be expressed in our laws; sometimes it is a matter of personal example, preference and good taste, whether in the words we use or the TV programmes we watch. Sometimes force of example counts for more than force of law. A Christian sense of social responsibility, expressed by personal example and the collective work and influence of the Church, remains an important part of Scottish life. It is a force for good in its thought, its faith and its work.

Our Church's contribution is both a major effort in practical social work and an opinion-forming rôle as described in the later chapter on Church and nation.

The Church and the universities

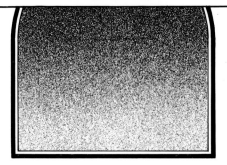

Scotland has eight universities and the Church has connections with all of them. All have chaplains who are mostly ministers of the Church of Scotland. All have staff and students belonging to the Church, often taking part in the evangelical Christian Unions, the Student Christian Movement, or in activities connected with the university chaplaincies. But the closest links with the Church are with the four older Scottish universities: three of which were founded by bishops before the Reformation (St Andrews, Glasgow and Aberdeen) and one (Edinburgh) founded a few years after the death of John Knox. It is in the Divinity faculties of these universities that the majority of the Kirk's ministers receive the academic side of their training. Among their professors are some of the leaders of the Church. Three Moderators of the General Assembly in the last ten years have been academic theologians holding Scottish chairs: Tom Torrance, Robin Barbour and John McIntyre. And many Divinity academics play a major part as members of Presbytery and Church boards and committees.

Until the 1960s the Divinity students of the Scottish universities were mainly candidates for the ministry of the Kirk. Many of them still are, although now there are more students than before from other denominations in Scotland and beyond; and there are even some (with varying degrees of success and satisfaction) who say that they study theology for its own sake, or as an intellectual discipline.

In this situation, some church leaders have argued that the Kirk needs a seminary (or at least a practical-theological finishing school) of its own, but they have not yet won over the General Assembly. Relations between parts of the Church and the universities are not always placid and untroubled, but each side respects the other's way of life and thought; neither is likely to seek a quarrel or a divorce. And the Kirk's Committee on Education for the Ministry (part of its Board of Education) co-operates closely with the universities.

In a sense the Kirk does have 'colleges', but, for practical purposes, they are very much the same thing as university faculties. St Andrews, the senior Scottish university, has a collegiate structure: it is St Mary's College which provides Divinity studies and training in this case. In Edinburgh, Glasgow and Aberdeen, however, the colleges (New College, Trinity College, and Christ's College respectively) are not ancient parts of the universities, but were absorbed into them after the Presbyterian reunion of 1929. They were once the colleges of the Free Church (later United Free) set up when a large part of the Kirk gave up its power and position (university chairs as well as parish manses) for the sake of conscience. The New College in Edinburgh, with the great Thomas Chalmers as its head, was quite literally that: the 'new college' of the Free Church.

During the reunion of the

Church of Scotland, these colleges and the Divinity faculties virtually merged, although their physical fates varied. Playfair's fine building on the Edinburgh Mound, down the stairway from the Assembly Hall, is still New College, but it houses the Divinity faculty and is now Edinburgh University's financial responsibility.

In Glasgow, the old Trinity College building has lain empty (there has been trouble finding a buyer) since teaching moved to the Glasgow university area at Gilmorehill. It remains, quite literally, a Victorian monument on the city's skyline, deserted and forlorn. But in Aberdeen, the neat Christ's College building (at the west end of Union Street) finds a modest usefulness and keeps a decent appearance.

There has always been a wide range of courses and types of students in the Divinity faculties. (On the other hand, not all ministers have degrees.) But many candidates only begin to study Divinity after a rigorous discipline and first degree in Arts or (less frequently) Science. Today, however, a Divinity degree may be a first degree, but courses can still be tailored to suit the needs of the Church and 'mature' candidates. Around 1960 signs indicated that pehaps in the future the majority of candidates would be 'mature', but now there is a fair range of ages with a large group of young candidates.

Older students come from many walks of life; some may have given up a Civil Service, or legal, or business career to take up their course. Some have also held positions in the armed forces. As mentioned earlier, there have even been much-publicised and quite exceptional cases put before the General Assembly concerning mature candidates for the ministry who had served prison sentences. It remains far more likely, however, that mature students will be converted tax-gatherers or personnel managers, rather than repentant criminals.

Candidates for the ministry pass or fail their Divinity degree according to the universities' rules, not the Church's. But the selection of candidates for the ministry is the Church's affair,

View of the Assembly Hall incorporating New College

not the universities'. The procedure is roughly similar to that of the Civil Service selection boards. Thereafter, the Church must approve candidates' courses and set requirements in practical work and Bible knowledge.

In 1984, the report to the General Assembly recorded that there had been 162 applications in the previous year (an all-time record) but that only 71 candidates had been accepted. There were then 178 students for the ministry in the four Scottish Divinity faculties, the spread being rather uneven; 62 at Glasgow, 59 at Edinburgh, 40 at Aberdeen (which has recently enjoyed a rising reputation), and only 17 at St Andrews. However, St Andrews has another 100 students from the British Isles, and beyond, taking theology degrees at St Mary's College. Other students (mainly prospective teachers) participate in some classes at the College as well. Some Divinity students may also become formal candidates for the ministry later, having started their university courses before applying to the Church or, perhaps, on being accepted by the Church's selection procedures. By 1985 the number of students training for the ministry had risen to 202.

In this time of economic pressure, which has affected all British universities, there have been hints and rumblings about 'concentration' on Divinity studies. The axe has fallen on the number of academic chairs and appointments, not the number of faculties; but this has been the problem of the universities in general, not of Divinity in particular. Perhaps there may be new problems and strains in the future, especially if there is a sustained, evangelical revival in the Church and a pronounced liberal, even radical, tendency in the Divinity faculties.

There may be other problems now that, in the West, the university world is not only inter-denominational, but international. This may mean that it is less likely for university teachers (or enough of them) to be available for the many duties which the Church likes to impose on them, if they are willing, as members of Presbyteries and committees. It also means that Scots ministers who become lecturers and want to become professors, may have to search for promotion in England, the overseas English-speaking world, or even continental Europe. For example, one of the most gifted younger Scottish theologians, Alastair Heron, was appointed to a chair at Erlangen in West Germany. This is not a new trend, especially in the English-speaking world. Several leading theologians in Scotland today have previously worked in the United States and Australia.

But the trend continues and must have some effect on the evolving relationship of the Church and the faculties.

Perhaps there has always been tension between universities (or colleges) and parts of the Church. As the academics see it, 'the universities will take account of, criticise, and interpret whatever seems important in theology and Church life'. But some people in the Church wonder whether some academic speculations are compatible with a biblical faith. But, the tension can be constructive, and for the good of the Church and universities alike.

Far round the world

The missionary tradition is as old as Christianity itself. It begins with Jesus's words about preaching the Gospel to all nations; teaching and baptising them. It began to influence Scotland, via Western Europe and Ireland, even before the end of the Roman Empire. Traders and soldiers may have brought the first 'Good News' but soon 'missionaries' were recognisable. Columba (a Scot from Ireland) and Ninian were missionaries. Scots missionaries established the faith among the Angles of Northern England. Indeed, many Scots and Irishmen have had an honourable place in the early Christian missions to Central Europe, and some of the resulting links have lasted a long time. Even today, there is *Schottenkirche* in Vienna; the name itself maintaining the mediæval connection.

The first 'overseas' work of the Reformed Scots Kirk was in Ireland. A Scots settlement of Ulster led to the establishment of Presbyterianism there, and eventually to the emergence of an Irish Church very close in style and affections to the Scots Kirk.

This Irish Church developed mainly in Ulster which is at times in sight of Scotland, situated as it is just across the water.

The Ulster Scots have had their ups and downs in the troubled history of Ireland; inclined at one time to the radicalism of the French Revolution and, in this century, to the populist conservatism characteristic of Ulster Protestantism. They have always had conservative and liberal wings, both politically and theologically. However, the Ulster-Scots were responsible, at least as much as the home Scots, for the development of an English-speaking Reformed religion of the Presbyterian style in what was later to become the United States of America. Many of these Scotch-Irish (as the Americans called them) took the side of General Washington in the revolutionary war (1775-1783). Before being absorbed into the main stream of American

evolution, they also played a distinctive part in the first great Westward move, although on the frontier, distinctions among Protestants came to have little significance and many Presbyterian-descended families were soon mingling happily with Methodists and many varieties of Baptist.

It was not until the days of the great Scots-Irish American, President Andrew Jackson, that the stay-at-home Scots Kirk was really captured by missionary enthusiasm. The first missionary, Alexander Duff, went to India in 1830. However the Scots Kirk always had its European connections; initially with Calvin, then with Holland in the turbulent 17th century. The Dutch attracted Scots students and gave political asylum. But in the age of imperial expansion, the Kirk looked across much more distant seas. Even then, however, many of its scholars went to Europe to study; this time to Germany.

There were two quite different kinds of Presbyterianism for export. The first involved the Scots who took their style of religion with them not only to the United States but to Australia, New Zealand and, on a smaller scale, to South Africa (where some of these Scots were to be absorbed among the Afrikaners) and even to Argentina. Most of the Scots were happy for a long time to be members of colonial congregations. Eventually they emerged in the English-speaking countries as Presbyterian Churches, although in this century, the majority of Australian and Canadian Presbyterians have merged into united churches. In South Africa, Scots had an influence in three very different strands of the Reformed tradition: missionaries created a black Presbyterian Church and English-speaking settlers a mainly white one, and the Dutch Reformed Church also owes much to the ministers from Scotland who learned to preach in Dutch and to speak its vernacular form, Afrikaans. The common ancestry and deep divisions are still obvious today.

The other stream of Presbyterianism for export came in the form of missionary enthusiasm to preach to the heathen; indeed not only to preach, but to set up Western-style schools and colleges, hospitals and even printing works. The first, and perhaps the greatest of the Scots Presbyterian missionaries, was Alexander Duff, who was to become a major influence on Indian education as well as Indian Christianity. During the Disruption, like most missionaries, he took the side of the Free Kirk. Soon, however, all the sections of Scots Presbyterianism were active in foreign missions, usually managing to keep out of each other's way. There was room for them all.

Some Scots also played a major part, especially in Africa, in the Independent, or Congregational, missionary tradition. There was not a very rigid division, even at home, between Congregationalism and some strains of Presbyterian secession. David Livingstone's father, for example, moved from the Kirk to the Independents (although, for his son, the turning point in his life was going to Africa under the London Missionary Society's (LMS) auspices and marrying into a Scots LMS missionary family: the Moffats).

The Scots effort was only part of a much wider Western movement, although generations of Scots were brought up with an understandably exaggerated idea of its success, whether in numbers of converts or its proportionate strength in relation to other Churches. But the Scots impact was considerable, and sometimes played a rôle in social, and even political, history quite disproportionate to the Presbyterian numerical strength. This was true, for example, in Nyasaland (now Malawi) and the South African Transkei and Ciskei, where the Lovedale Mission pioneered higher education for blacks. In some of these countries (Malawi, South Africa and Kenya, for example) the missions have evolved into significant Presbyterian Churches that still maintain their Scottish partnerships. In other countries (such as North and South India, and Zambia) the Scots tradition remains an important element in the history of united Protestant Churches which found the

The congregation at Lovedale District Church

European denominational divisions scarcely relevant in their situations.

This ecumenical process was especially marked after the important missionary conference in Edinburgh in 1910. It was held in the Assembly Hall; then belonging to the United Free Church and now the setting for the Church of Scotland General Assembly. That conference is often seen as the first really dramatic manifestation of the ecumenical movement. It set in motion the developments which led to the creation of the World Council of Churches in 1948, with the Church of Scotland among the founder-members. It exhibited a considerable influence in comparison to its modest size. Even now, at a time of Third World influence (perhaps even dominance) in the WCC's policy-making, the Kirk's rôle remains substantial, as it still does in the World Alliance of Reformed Churches, also based in Geneva.

Today the world-wide missionary partnership remains but the missionary effort is on a reduced scale. (It is also no

Opposite: *Missionaries abroad*

longer just a one-way traffic: Indian or Korean or African 'missionaries' come to the West). In Third World countries, Western Christians cannot assume their previous colonial rôles anymore. In the East, the Chinese Church has evolved in directions determined not by ecumenical conferences, but by the strains of war and adversity. Even India can be reluctant to let ministers from abroad have work permits. Remaining white missionaries in Africa have to be sensitive in political matters. This applies particularly in the countries where 'majority rule' may have resulted in an authoritarian or unstable government, but it is perhaps a natural and inevitable response in any young country where foreigners could become involved in political issues.

Nevertheless, a substantial number of people (ministers and laymen and women) go from Scotland on missionary service abroad, although rarely for the life-long overseas work undertaken by most of the earlier missionaries.

Thus the Scots missionary effort has found an honourable place in Christian history. The connections it has established will play their part in the universal Church's future. They are still being extended and renewed in the modern partnership of Churches, and in the two-way movement of mission and missionaries.

There was also a mission, not to the heathen, which had an honourable place in Church history despite the low number of converts it won: the mission to the Jews. From 1839, when the Scots ministers, Andrew Bonar and Robert McCheyne, made and recorded a memorable journey to Jerusalem (even then the 'centre of the Jewish world'), until about

Robert Murray McCheyne 1813-43

the Second World War, the mission to the Jews was of major importance to a section of the Church, and it had lasting results, quite apart from having a dramatic effect on individual lives. It provided a background of sympathy and understanding for a different kind of Christian-Jewish dialogue; the other was to establish a Scots presence in the Holy Land, even although the actual building of the Scots Kirk in Jerusalem, looking across the valley to Mount Zion, was undertaken not as a missionary enterprise, but as a memorial to the Scots who fell in the British First World War campaign which drove the Turks out of Palestine. Before that, however, there had been already a strong Scots impact at Tiberias and in Jaffa.

Perhaps no country has shown as clearly as the Holy Land in the past century how dramatically both the environment and the nature of a Christian mission may change. The changes may take unexpected forms and the future may be unpredictable, but some good seed may still, as in the Parable of the Sower, spring up and increase.

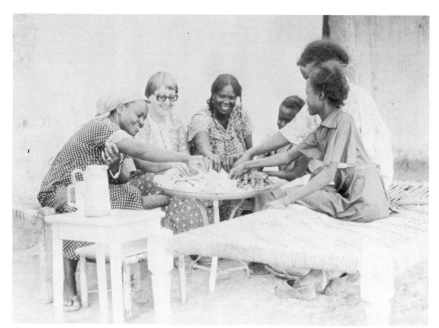

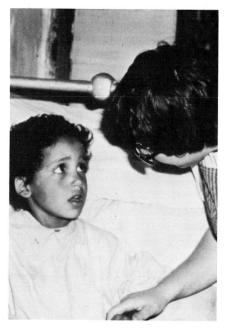

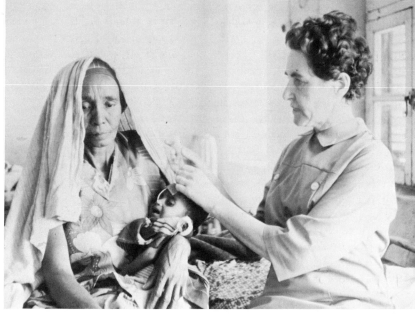

The Kirk abroad

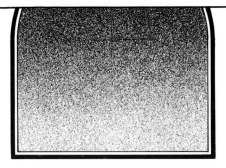

The main legacy left by the overseas missions of the Church of Scotland is to be found in the Churches which have taken over from the missionaries or from the 'colonial' congregations. These Churches are influenced by their respective cultures in much the same way as our Kirk is.

But the Kirk still has a network of overseas congregations, especially in Europe, whose main rôle is to provide churches for Scots living abroad, and for people from other countries who find the Scots style of worship congenial. In some of these 'Scots churches', the majority of the congregation may be from other countries. Often, they are English-speaking ex-patriates. In recent times, recruits to these congregations have come from a wider geographical range, including Korea and Ghana (and other African countries).

There are also some Scots congregations in England; two of them in London. The larger is St Columba's in Pont Street, close to Harrods. The other is Crown Court in Covent Garden. The 'Presbytery of England' also includes two Scots congregations

in the Northamptonshire town of Corby, a large part of whose population was composed of immigrant Scots steelworkers. There are also small congregations in Newcastle, Gillingham and Liverpool, and substantial ones in Jersey and Guernsey which decided to come into the Church of Scotland a few years ago, although their own Reformed tradition dates back to the 16th century. There are Scots congregations in Carlisle and Berwick as well, but these are treated as parts of the adjoining Scots Presbytery areas.

The present Scots congregations in Europe are to be found in Amsterdam, Rotterdam, Brussels, Geneva, Lausanne, Malta, Rome, Paris, Lisbon and Gibraltar (which also serves Scots in Southern Spain, depending upon current political conditions). Links with the old 'colonial' tradition of the Kirk are still found in Bermuda, The

Bahamas, Trinidad and Sri Lanka (Ceylon), with each congregation evolving to suit local needs and conditions. There is also a 'Presbytery of Jerusalem' with two churches: one is St Andrew's, Jerusalem; the other is at Tiberias on the Sea of Galilee. Both have adjacent hospices. Tabeetha School at Jaffa is run by the Church of Scotland, although its pupils come from many countries and are members of several religions.

Other Scots connections can be found in Hungary (where what was once a Jewish mission now provides English services in co-operation with the Hungarian Reformed Church) and in Argentina, where Scots-Argentinians are inevitably moving closer to other Reformed Churches in the country. There is even a congregation in Chile which remains linked to the Kirk.

Wherever there is a Scots community the Kirk can still meet a need. For example, there are now more Kirk members in Southern Spain than in Gibraltar, and suggestions about future needs have ranged from West Germany to the Oil States.

Church and nation

It has never been easy to draw a neat line separating practical politics from applied religion. With hindsight, it is possible to see times, even in the history of the Scots Kirk, when the Christian Church has been drawn too far into contemporary political controversies; times when the Church has been so pious and unwordly that it did less than it should and could have done to create more fairness and justice.

There are three kinds of Christian involvement in public matters of political concern which are reflected in the life of the Kirk. All of them are quite free of any party attachment, although there are inevitably members of the Kirk who are active and leading members in all our democratic political parties. First, there are Christian values which the Church is anxious to see reflected, sustained and developed in society. Second, there are matters which the Kirk has to face as a Scottish institution, concerning the way in which Scotland is governed, and the way that economic or social policies affect Scottish life. Third,

there are immediate affairs where the local church or the area Presbytery voices the concerns and feelings of the community.

At national level, the main demonstration of such concern is shown by the Church and Nation Committee of the General Assembly, and the proceedings on Church and Nation day at the General Assembly when its report is considered, often with new ideas and proposals being added from the floor of the House. On that day, debates may range from the ethics of the Bomb via the effects of a factory closure, to anxiety about fishing limits, or even about drivers' disregard of speed restrictions on the road. (Although the Kirk is sometimes told that it needs an accelerator and not a Moderator!)

However, some matters of national importance with political implications come through the Assembly debates and committee activities on education and social

responsibility. On these 'Church and Nation' and related matters, the Kirk is not only far from infallible, but can also be far from united!

There are, however, some fairly constant factors in the Kirk's affairs. One is the concern for peace, usually with some division about the best means of keeping it. This division was particularly evident in the debates of the 1930s about pacifism (even although some of the pacifists were decorated ex-combatants of 1914-18) and this issue has been revived in a more contemporary form in the modern debate about unilateral nuclear disarmament. The emphasis and wording of the General Assembly debate varies, reflecting the strength of the pacifist, or 'nuclear pacifist', minority and the difficulty it finds in carrying the rest of the Church with it.

This international concern also finds strong expression in support of human rights in very different parts of the world, and in support of overseas aid and world development issues. Another constant factor for concern is family life. Yet another is the anxiety about the strength and stability of the Scottish economy in an age of rapid technological change. This, for example, has made the Kirk a powerful influence in lobbying against the threatened closure of the Ravenscraig steel-works, and in support of peace in the pits.

Many Kirk members and most of the Church and Nation Committee would also like to consider as a constant factor for their concern, the need for a form of government which allows a fuller expression of Scottish identity within the United Kingdom. This has been the view of the General Assembly. (Nationalists might delete the words 'within the United Kingdom'.) Many other Kirk members, even while agreeing to the proposition in principle, tend to question the particular political proposals aimed at expressing it. For example, the Church and National Committee seemed to support a 'Yes' vote at the Scottish devolution referendum in 1979. Many people in the Kirk objected, and analysis of the results suggests that the ordinary members may have been evenly split; perhaps with a small majority voting 'No'. No-one can be sure how the General Assembly would have voted if it had met at the height of that campaign.

To some extent Kirk members also express their preferences by showing their interest (or lack of interest) in the political aspect of the Church's community involvement. Sometimes a left-right division is fairly apparent, but so far it has never been defined well enough to be a hindrance to the Church's mission or its sense of community. Indeed, political concerns have helped to inspire an acute awareness of the human cost of high unemployment.

There are also very distinct differences, sometimes of emphasis, or occasionally of opinion, on social questions. The Assembly, for example, periodically gives the impression that it has stopped just short of urging members to be teetotal. But the 'total abstinence' tradition in Scots Presbyterianism is a strong minority view, not a ruling of the Church. After all, whisky itself is sometimes called 'a drop of the Auld Kirk'! The consensus in the Kirk, however (and one that has been recently gaining specialist support outside) is that Scotland pays a heavy price for its heavy drinking and alcohol abuse. Now, with practical help as well as warnings, the Church takes a leading rôle in facing up to threats from even deadlier drugs.

The Assembly also discourages gambling in society; even the mildest forms are not supposed to be found in church bazaars and sales of work. (In fact they sometimes are, despite a prohibition. People have been known to win a bottle of whisky in a church tombola!) But the ethos of the modern Scots Protestant, in the Kirk and outside, is that moral decisions are essentially individual ones. This has guided the Kirk's thinking on many family matters, like birth control, for example.

The Kirk is not, at least in modern times, a strongly authoritarian Church, but one that wants to see personal and social moral attitudes guided by the concept of Christian freedom. But this approach may have to be altered in a society where Christians often feel like a minority group, and where a different concept of freedom may prevail. Whether abuse of this freedom (not only in drink and gambling, but in matters of marriage, sex, and family life) will bring about a powerful puritan reaction, remains to be seen. Perhaps, on the other hand, we shall find our way to a new and compassionate style of puritanism, even if the word, as well as the concept, still needs to be rehabilitated.

The Scots, and especially the Presbyterians, have a reputation for puritanism, although this reputation never entirely stands up to a close investigation of pub life on a Saturday night. It is arguable that Scots go to extremes, both in puritanism and in anti-puritan reaction. Perhaps the two tendencies can even be found in the same individuals! After all, our national poet, Robert Burns, was the author of bawdy verses, the appraiser of 'bold John Barleycorn', as well as the creator of the pious verses of *The Cottar's Saturday Night*.

Nowadays, the Scottish reputation for plain living and high thinking may not stand up to the pressures of a smaller and changing world. It is not easy to know how significantly the international media influence tastes and habits, or how far they merely reflect them. But the Church, with different emphases provided by the various groups within it, will remain a force in favour of things that are 'lovely and of good report'.

Postscript

The Kirk's future

The gates of Hell will not prevail against the Church, Jesus said (*Matthew 16:18*). The great modern scholar and communicator of the Kirk, William Barclay, rendered those words of Jesus from Matthew's Gospel thus: 'The powers of death will be helpless to harm it.' And we have the assurance too, from the same Gospel, that where even two or three people are gathered in the name of Jesus, He will be among them.

It is in the light of these assurances that our Church faces an unknown future as an institution. This is not an age where people admire or revere institutions. They are suspicious of them and especially resentful of those that claim authority. The Church has learned the dangers of claiming the kinds of authority which are all too easily corrupted by the inclinations and processes which Christians call sin. All too often in Christian history the claim to authority in God's name has gone against what God actually showed through Jesus.

But the Church is an 'institution'; not only to work effectively, but also to ensure that it is there to meet people's needs. It has (so it believes) been founded by Jesus; sometimes betraying Him (as Peter did in Jerusalem), often failing to show the love He showed, and all too often reflecting the failures of its very fallible leaders and ordinary members. Yet despite all this, the Church still survives the attacks of the 'powers of death' which are partially within it (because they are within all of us), and the other powers which attack the Church from the outside.

Our Church's future might be easier to plan if those attacks were crude and cruel, like the persecutions many Christians experience elsewhere in the world. Indifference is a subtler enemy and the main one in Scotland: one that threatens Christians with frustration rather than martyrdom. But even indifference has no resistance to 'the powers of death'. Indeed, it is the fact of death, and the true perspective it gives to our lives, that ultimately limits the power of indifference. In officially atheist countries today, it is the response of Christians to death and suffering (not just persecution, but the suffering that material or medical progress cannot abolish) that makes nonsense of the prophecies that religion will wither away.

It will not. In every culture, the Christian faith will respond not only to new ideas, discoveries and experiences, but to the other kinds of experience which are rooted in the history of a people, as the Kirk is in Scotland. There will be new growth from the old roots.

We in the Church may feel this as an act of faith. But one of the discoveries of the secular world today is that there is far more continuity in national life than the creators of revolutions realise. In many ways we live, even in Scotland, in an age of revolution: a cultural, social, scientific revolution of rapidly and dramatically changing customs, manners and tastes. To all these changes the Kirk must respond, and there will be obvious and sometimes lively arguments among us about our responses, which might range from new styles of evangelism and 'old-time religion' to a Kirk-sponsored project, studying the relation of 'society, religion, and technology'.

We are a coalition Church, tolerant and flexible. That gives us a lot of strength but also many weaknesses. However, it is a fact of our past history and present experience that very different styles of Christianity will be accommodated within our Presbyterian order. Other predictions cannot be so confidently made. We can only list possibilities, some probabilities, the occasional certainty: probably the Kirk will remain Presbyterian in its present form, despite the arguments for some kind of bishops in the presbytery as part of an attempt at a wider ecumenical unity; probably membership will fall for some years yet before stabilising and then possibly increasing; probably the number of churches will stabilise sooner than the membership roll, especially if

there is a major extension in the use of part-time ('auxiliary') ministers, lay preachers ('readers'), and of elders in new rôles.

Certainly the Kirk will retain its parish system which tries to reach and serve the whole of Scotland. Probably, despite the 'new forms of ministry', the chaplaincies, community experiments and so on, the parish minister will remain the key man or woman in the Church's leadership. Certainly the Kirk will develop closer relations with other Churches and add to the number of local arrangements which involve ecumenical co-operation. Possibly it will be involved in minor but useful acts of Church union in Scotland; in effect absorbing some smaller kindred Protestant groups, who will contribute their own styles and traditions. Possibly it will come under strain as its Evangelical wing (apparently gaining in strength) disagrees with its liberals who appear to dilute or radically re-interpret traditional Christian doctrine. But this tension is likely to reflect much wider Christian

arguments, such as the one in the Church of England involving the Bishop of Durham's presentation of his beliefs, and the friction in the Roman Church over 'liberation theology'. It is possible, but far less likely than in the last century, that these arguments may take a distinctively Scottish form.

But it is not our duty to worry too much about the future. Christians are people who ought to live and work in the time God has given them with the assurance that the future is in God's hands and that, as St Paul said in his *Letter to the Romans,* all things work together for the good of them that love God. William Barclay put that passage in a contemporary idiom: 'We know that through the work of the Spirit all the different events of life are being made to work for good for those who keep on loving God'. (*Letter to Romans, New Testament translation, Collins.*) For those, that is, who are called according to God's purposes. We are not so arrogant in our Church to think that we always know God's purposes.

We who make up the Kirk

of Scotland today know only too well our failures and inadequacies. We are poorer in spirit than many of those who have gone before us and will come after us. But we have not lost our sense of the sovereignty of God and the unique, saving grace demonstrated to us through Jesus. There is still reassurance for us in the insight that made the Burning Bush our emblem (*Exodus 3:2*). It was aflame with fire, but not consumed.

We are not worshippers of history; but we see the God we worship working in history, before and since that intervention in history that came with the first Christmas. We are of the universal Church of Christ; and in this rough and hilly country of Scotland, we are a Church that has seen human frailty and weakness shaped, turned and inspired to God's purposes.

Ours is the Church of Ninian and Columba; of Knox and the Reformers; of the Covenanting martyrs hounded in the bleak moorlands; of the philosophical moderates and missionary evangelicals; of Thomas Chalmers and Norman Macleod in one century and George MacLeod in another. Perhaps none of these people, when they made their impact on Scotland and the Scottish Church, knew any more than we do today about the future of the Church and the nation.

Now there are many things we see only as dim images in a mirror (through a glass darkly, is the more classical form of Paul's phrase) and our gifts of knowledge and inspired messages are only partial. A time will come, no-one knows when, for the completion of all things: meanwhile faith, hope and love remain. It is on these elements, all derived from Jesus, that His Kirk in Scotland is founded. The future is His, not ours. As one of our Scots paraphrases says of the greatest of these three qualities: 'He loved us from the first of time, He loves us to the last.' We believe that nothing can separate us from the love of God. And if that is so, we should *work* for the future of our Church, and spend less time worrying about it.

Appendix 1: Church structures

The life of the Church of Scotland is far more interesting than its structures but here are some facts for those who want them.

The General Assembly of the Kirk meets annually in the second half of May, starting on a Saturday and ending the following Friday.

The Church is organised into 46 Presbyteries of varying sizes in Scotland; plus the Presbytery of England, the Presbytery of Europe and the Presbytery of Jerusalem. The last three provide a Presbyterian structure for congregations outside Scotland which are part of the Scots Kirk and not local Reformed Churches.

For some purposes Presbyteries are grouped into 12 Synods.

The central administrative offices of the Church are located at 121 George Street, Edinburgh, near Charlotte Square.

The central work of the Church is carried out on behalf of the General Assembly by various boards, committees, trusts and panels. The main ones are:

Board of Practice and Procedure

Board of Ministry and Mission

Board of Social Responsibility (the Kirk's Social Work Department)

Board of World Mission and Unity

Board of Communication

Board of Education

Board of Stewardship and Finance

Assembly Council (not quite an executive but more a co-ordinating committee)

Church and Nation Committee

General Trustees (with responsibility for buildings)

Panel on Doctrine

Panel on Worship

The Woman's Guild reports to the General Assembly as a committee but has a network of its own, with Presbyterial councils as well as local branches.

At any given time, there are also likely to be a number of *ad hoc* committees or commissions preparing reports for the General Assembly or having delegated powers to act on its behalf.

Reports to the 1985 General Assembly showed:

887 165 communicant members in Scotland

1765 congregations served by 1348 ministers

46 223 elders

21 276 baptisms in 1983, of which 1769 were adults

12 345 new members admitted in 1984 by 'profession of faith'

There were nearly 23 000 Sunday school teachers and just under 140 000 children in Sunday school and Bible classes. About 131 000 boys and girls were in Church-linked youth organisations and clubs.

Total income in 1984 was £46 148 971, of which £37 083 147 was congregational income. The balance included bequests, investment income, sales of property, etc. Nearly 140 000 members give by deed of covenant.

Appendix 2: A glossary of the Kirk

Adherent: An adult, connected with a congregation and (usually) attending worship, who is not enrolled as a communicant member. In parts of the Highlands and Islands most church-goers remain adherents and membership figures are misleading. The Kirk is thought to have nearly 50 000 such adherents.

Assembly: Abbreviation for The General Assembly.

Auld Kirk: A term for the part of the Church which remained as the 'Establishment' (after the 1843 split, now healed). Also a nickname for whisky.

Auxiliary Minister: A minister ordained for local service, but pursuing a 'lay' trade or profession (or retired from it). Originally to be called 'non-stipendiary' ministers. The first auxiliaries were ordained in 1984.

Baptism: The sacrament of admission to the Christian community, as in the christening of believers' children. But adults are also baptised when joining the Church if they have not been baptised in infancy.

Barrier Act: A Kirk law (dating from 1697) requiring major changes in the Church of Scotland to be put to Presbyteries for approval as well as the General Assembly. A special procedure involving two different references to Presbyteries (in successive years), a two-thirds vote among Presbyteries, and further Assembly approval, applies to the basic 'constitution' set out in *The Declaratory Articles* (q.v.).

Bible: The Scriptures of the Old and New Testament. Several translations are now used in the Kirk. The *Apocrypha* is not usually printed with Bibles used in Scotland, except for some New English Bible editions.

Bishops: The Kirk does not have these officers, except in so far as parish ministers approximate to New Testament bishops. But the term is affectionately applied to ministers when training and guiding probationary ministers.

Board: The main national administrative committees of the General Assembly are now called boards. Locally the term applies to boards of management which, in many congregations (not all), handle finances and buildings.

Burning Bush, The: The bush which burned yet 'was not consumed' (Exodus 3:2) is the badge or emblem of the Church of Scotland — adopted first, it is said, from the French Huguenots.

Call: In general terms, this denotes the prospective minister's sense of his mission or 'calling'. In more particular terms, the invitation to a minister to take up a particular appointment.

Cathedral: In the Church of Scotland the name has no legal significance but is applied to certain historic churches, among them *Glasgow Cathedral, St Giles'* in Edinburgh, *St Magnus* in Kirkwall, and *Dunblane Cathedral.*

Church and Nation: This Committee makes most of the Kirk's pronouncements on political matters and reports to the General Assembly on them. Only the Assembly can actually declare the mind of the Church.

Commissioners: Name given to members of the General Assembly. (But see *Lord High Commissioner*). Presbyteries appoint them.

Commission of Assembly: A body able to act for the Assembly between its annual meetings. Until recently it met in October and February (with all the previous Assembly invited) but these regular meetings have been discontinued.

Communion: The sacrament of the Lord's Supper. In general the Kirk's people apply the term to the whole service in which Communion is a part (and in which the Word is preached), not just to the procedures of sharing the bread and wine which re-enact The Last Supper of Jesus and his disciples. 'Attendance at Communion' is often seen as a rough guide to whether Kirk members are active or have lapsed.

Confession: The Kirk does not have 'auricular confession', and its members confess their sins to God, not priests. 'The Confession' generally means the *Westminster Confession of Faith*. See also *Scots Confession.*

Covenant: Historically a solemn

association to defend or advance Reformed principles in the nation (using the biblical term applied to God's Covenant with His people).

Cox: The colloquial name for the standard guide to the practice and procedures of the Kirk, by Dr James Cox, 1934. The present revised version is the sixth edition.

Deacons (Deaconesses, Diaconate): From the 1880s the Kirk had an order of specially commissioned women, often serving as social workers in the Church or in Christian education, pastoral care and evangelism. There is now provision for a diaconate of both sexes but the deaconesses retain the old name. In some congregations with a Free Church ancestry the term *deacon* is given to those who handle the temporal business of the Church.

Declaratory Articles, The: The constitution of the Church of Scotland, setting out its doctrinal position (in very general terms) and its legal position.

Deliverance: A resolution (notably of the General Assembly).

Disruption, The: The division of the historic Church of Scotland in 1843, when a Free Church was formed by those who left the Established Church.

Elder: Person ordained (after election) to share in the rule and pastoral care of the church as a member of the local kirk session and possibly higher courts. But ministers are often thought of as 'teaching elders', as distinct from ordinary or 'ruling' elders.

Eucharist: 'Thanksgiving' — a Greek word for The Lord's Supper or Communion. It is used ecumenically to avoid talking about The Lord's Supper or the Mass where these terms are thought divisive.

Free Kirk: The Free Church of Scotland (See *'Wee Frees'*) in the tradition of the minority who stayed out of the 1900 union creating the United Free Church.

Free Presbyterians: A small, mainly Highland, ultra-Calvinist Church, separate from the Free Kirk.

Freewill Offering: A regular commitment to a weekly (or monthly) contribution to the Church, usually put in a 'freewill offering envelope'.

General Assembly, The: The national supreme court and parliament of the Scots Church, meeting in Edinburgh each May. It is about 1200 strong (plus delegates and visitors) and composed equally of ministers and elders representing Presbyteries.

Guild, The: Abbreviation for the Kirk's Woman's Guild.

Iona Community: A society within the Church, now ecumenical in membership, founded by George MacLeod (later Lord MacLeod of Fuinary) in 1938. It did much to restore Iona Abbey, although some of the society's work is based in Glasgow. It has a strong political interest; generally seen as left-of-centre and pacifist-inclined. Its aim is to express the theology of the Incarnation in social terms.

Kirk Session: The governing council of a congregation or parish in spiritual things and sometimes also temporal church affairs. (Some sessions have no separate boards for financial management.)

Layman, laywoman: In the Kirk the words are used colloquially, not theologically.

Lay Missionary: As used in the Kirk the term applies to full-time pastoral workers who are, in effect, assistant ministers but unordained.

Licentiate: A person qualified to preach and to be ordained as a minister (although not yet ordained and therefore unable to administer the sacraments). Many licentiates are also probationers, completing practical training for the ministry.

'Life and Work': The national magazine of the Church of Scotland, founded by a great Victorian Auld Kirker, A H Charteris, in 1879, but since 1930 adding the sub-heading *The Record of the Church of Scotland* as a result of a merger with the former United Free Church's *Record*.

Lines: Colloquial term for a certificate of transference from one congregation to another. When a member leaves one congregation and joins another this is called 'lifting your lines'.

Lord High Commissioner: The Crown's representative at (not in) the Assembly, in the absence of the Monarch. He (or she) sits in a gallery above the proceedings but customarily addresses the Assembly only at the beginning and end of the proceedings. The LHC usually stays at the Palace of Holyroodhouse and offers much hospitality, the most notable event being a garden party.

Manse: The house, usually a tied house, of the minister. Similar to an English rectory or vicarage.

Member: In a sense all baptised persons are church members but the term is usually applied to 'full' members or communicants on the congregational roll.

Minister: A Reformed clergyman (or woman), best regarded as a priest only in the sense in which all Christian believers share priesthood, but ordained to the ministry of Word and Sacraments.

Missionary: Usually applied, except in the case of 'lay missionaries' in Scotland, to Church workers, whether ministers or not, serving with churches overseas.

Moderator: Chairman (or woman) of a Church court, notably the chair-minister of the Assembly. For the next year he (or she) acts as a church spokesman and touring dignitary. Theoretically an elder could also be elected. However, in Presbyteries and Synods the minister in the chair is also called a moderator, as is the local minister when chairing the kirk session.

Netherbow: The Church's arts centre on Edinburgh's 'Royal Mile', next to John Knox's House.

Ordination: Principally the admission of a person to the ministry of Word and Sacraments. It is for life, and ministers are inducted, not re-ordained, when they move to a new parish. The term

is also properly used in the Kirk (although frowned upon in some esoteric ministerial circles) for the commitment of elders, which is also for life. When they move they can be 'admitted' to a new session.

Paraphrases: Commonly applied to hymns which are 'passages of Scripture paraphrased'.

Parish: Obsolete as a civil unit of local government. But each church of the Kirk has a territorial parish to which it has special responsibilities. In country districts these are often the traditional parishes.

Presbyter: There are two different usages. Often applied to all members of Presbyteries (ministers and elders) but sometimes (from a 'higher' Church position) applied to ministers and, in other Churches, priests. This usage, official in South India, does not suit Scottish conditions.

Presbytery: The Kirk's regional court and government, consisting of the ministers of the area in active Church service (or retired from it, or in other special rôles); of elders representing their congregations; and of those 'freely elected' to match the numbers of ministers without parishes.

Procurator: A lawyer (advocate) who is in effect the Kirk's standing senior counsel, often referred to on legal matters at the General Assembly. He is distinct from the Church's senior staff solicitor who handles day-to-day legal matters.

Profession: Commitment, notably in the 'profession of faith' required of new

members in joining the Church, as communicant members.

Psalms: In Scotland this is generally taken to mean the Scots metrical Psalms. The Psalms in the Bible are referred to as 'prose Psalms'.

Queen, The: The sovereign takes an oath on accession to uphold the rights and Presbyterian government of the Church of Scotland. When in Scotland, the Queen has ministers of the Kirk as her chaplains. It is wrong to call the Queen the head of the Church of Scotland, although London newspapers sometimes do so!

Reader: A 'lay preacher' in the Kirk.

Reformed: All Protestant Churches are in a sense 'Reformed' but the term applies especially to Presbyterian and Congregational Churches in the Calvinist tradition (as distinct from the Lutheran and Anglican ones).

Reverend: Adjective used to describe ministers: e.g. the Reverend (or Rev.) John Smith — never 'Rev. Smith'.

Right Reverend: The honorific (not legal) title adopted by the Moderator of the General Assembly while in office.

Saint Andrew Press, The: The Kirk's publishing house.

Scots Confession, The: The manifesto (1560) of the Scottish Reformation, setting out the faith of Scots Protestants. Sometimes called *John Knox's Confession*.

Stipend: A minister's pay, which includes the provision of a manse (q.v.) or, less often, a manse allowance. In 1985 the minimum stipend was £7140 plus a manse.

Synod: A church court, with little function in the modern Kirk, consisting of a group of Presbyteries, and situated between them and the General Assembly.

Table (or Holy Table): The correct term for the 'altar' in Reformed worship.

United Free (UF): The name of the Church formed in 1900 by the union of the great majority of the Free Church with the United Presbyterians (see below). It united with the Established Church of Scotland in 1929, with a very small part continuing (as it does today) as a separate Church.

United Presbyterians (UP): A Church formed in 1847 which merged into the United Free Church in 1900. It united Presbyterians whose churches derived from various secessions. It was closer to Congregationalism than most Presbyterian Churches, and some modern Kirk congregations retain the 'UP constitution' which limited the power of minister and Presbytery.

Very Reverend: Honorific title used by custom (not law) for former moderators of the General Assembly (and Deans of the Thistle, and Principals of *St Mary's College,* St Andrews).

'Wee Frees': The part of the Free Church of Scotland which did not join the union of 1900 and won the right to keep the name in law. Still strong in the Highlands and Islands.

Westminster Confession, The: The statement of Calvinist Reformed belief adopted in England, with Scots help, during the civil war against Charles I, and still the 'principal subordinate standard' (next to the Bible) of the Church of Scotland.

World Alliance of Reformed Churches: The Presbyterian and Congregational equivalent of Anglican and Lutheran international organisations. Geneva-based, in the same building as the World Council of Churches offices. The Church of Scotland is a founder-member.

World Council of Churches: World-wide, organisation which includes most Churches (Roman Catholics and some conservative Protestants excepted). The Church of Scotland is a founder-member.

Index

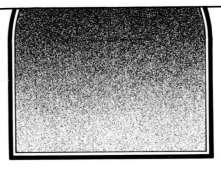